MISSOURI

impressions | photography by Scott R. Avetta

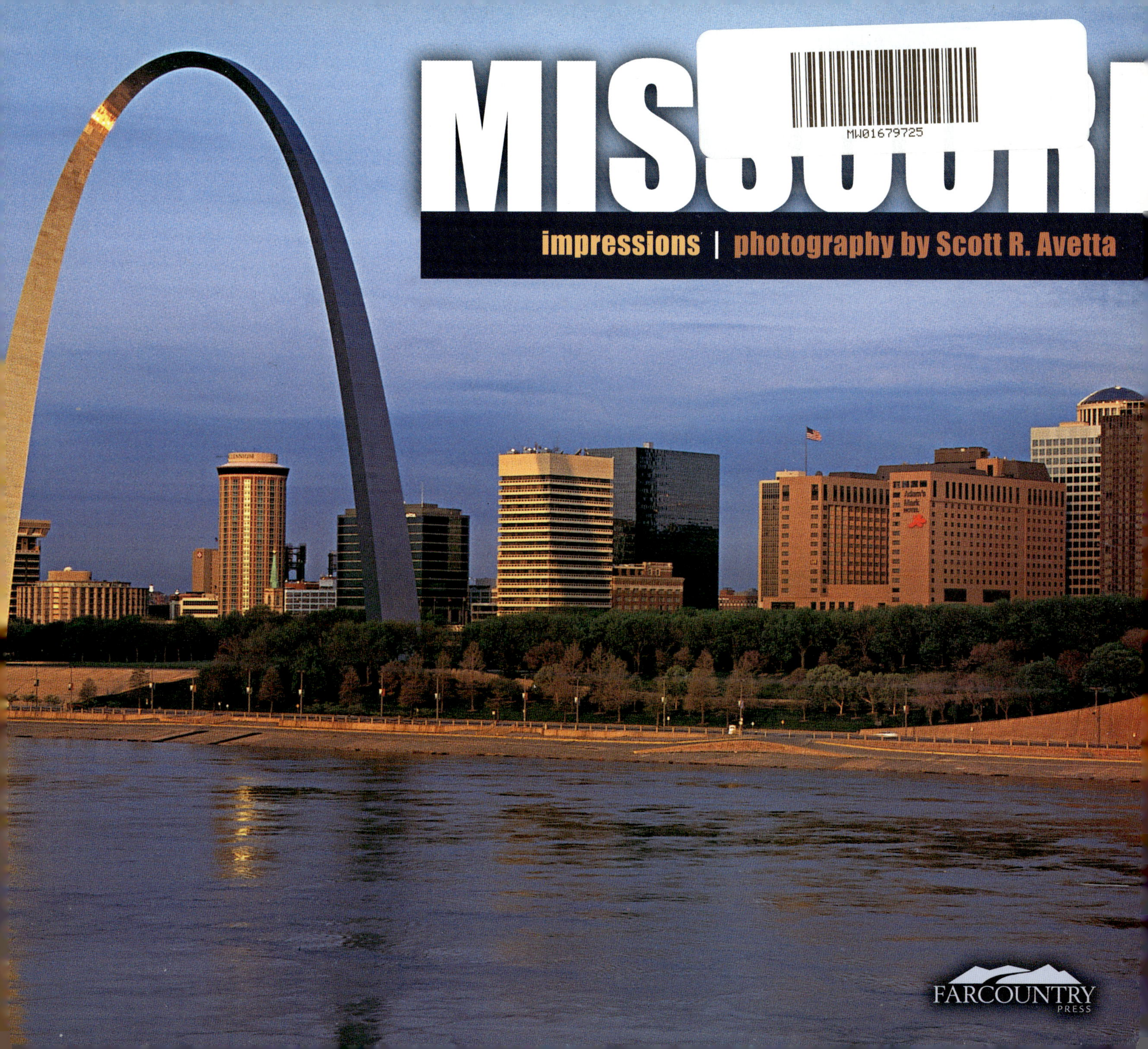

FARCOUNTRY PRESS

Right: Early risers who stroll along the Missouri River, pictured here in Herman, are often enveloped in the golden glow of sunrise.

Title page: The Gateway Arch on the banks of the Mississippi River symbolizes St. Louis's position as the historic entrance to the West.

Cover: Missouri chose the flowering dogwood as its state tree in 1955. These lovely spring blossoms will produce bright red fruits by autumn

Back cover: Pleasure boaters chug across Lake of the Ozarks, seen from a popular overlook on a bluff at Ha Ha Tonka State Park, near the shell of the old castle.

ISBN 10: 1-56037-475-6
ISBN 13: 978-1-56037-475-6

For more information about our books, write Farcountry Press, P.O. Box 5630, Helena, MT 59604; call (800) 821-3874; or visit www.farcountrypress.com.

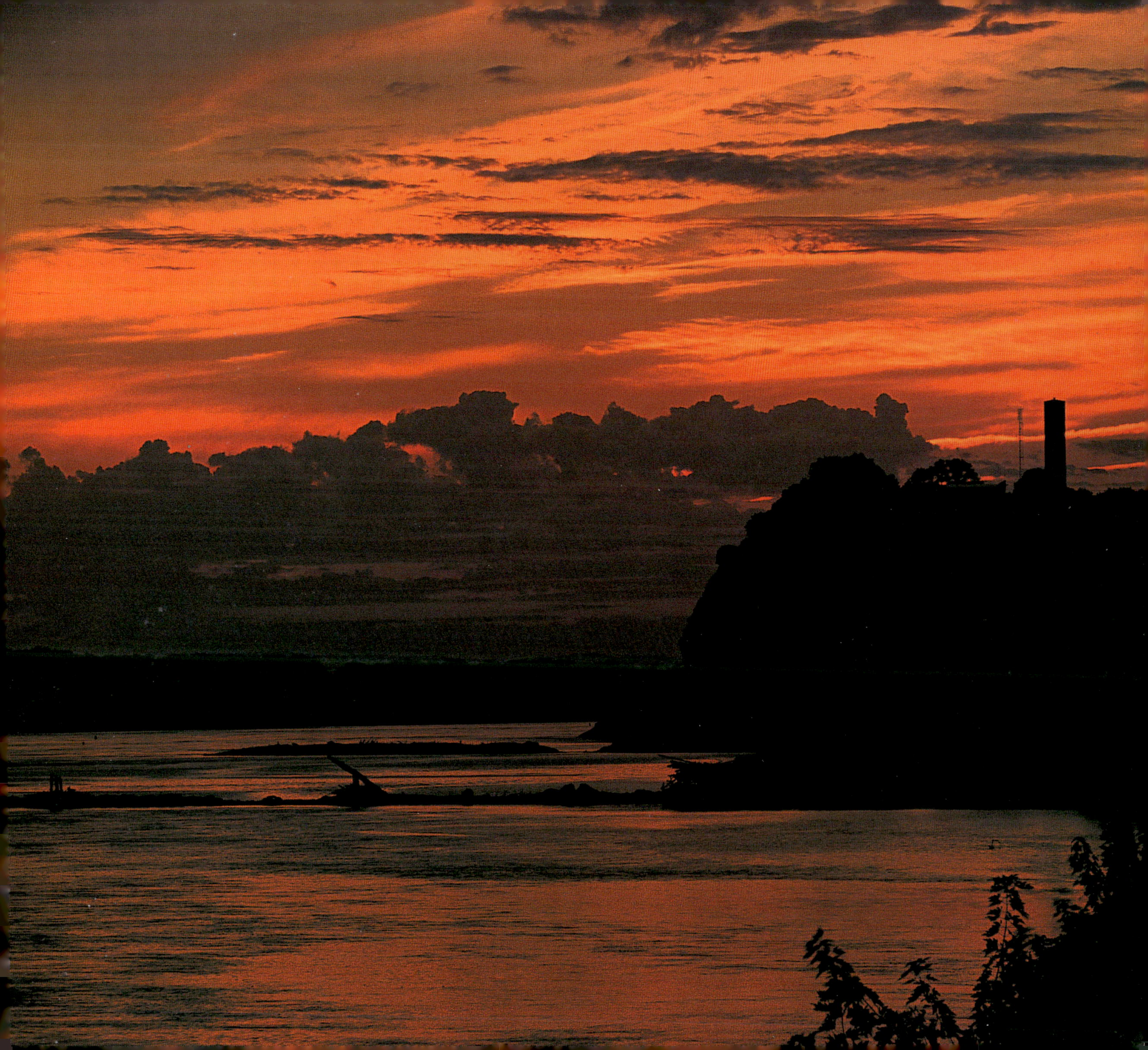

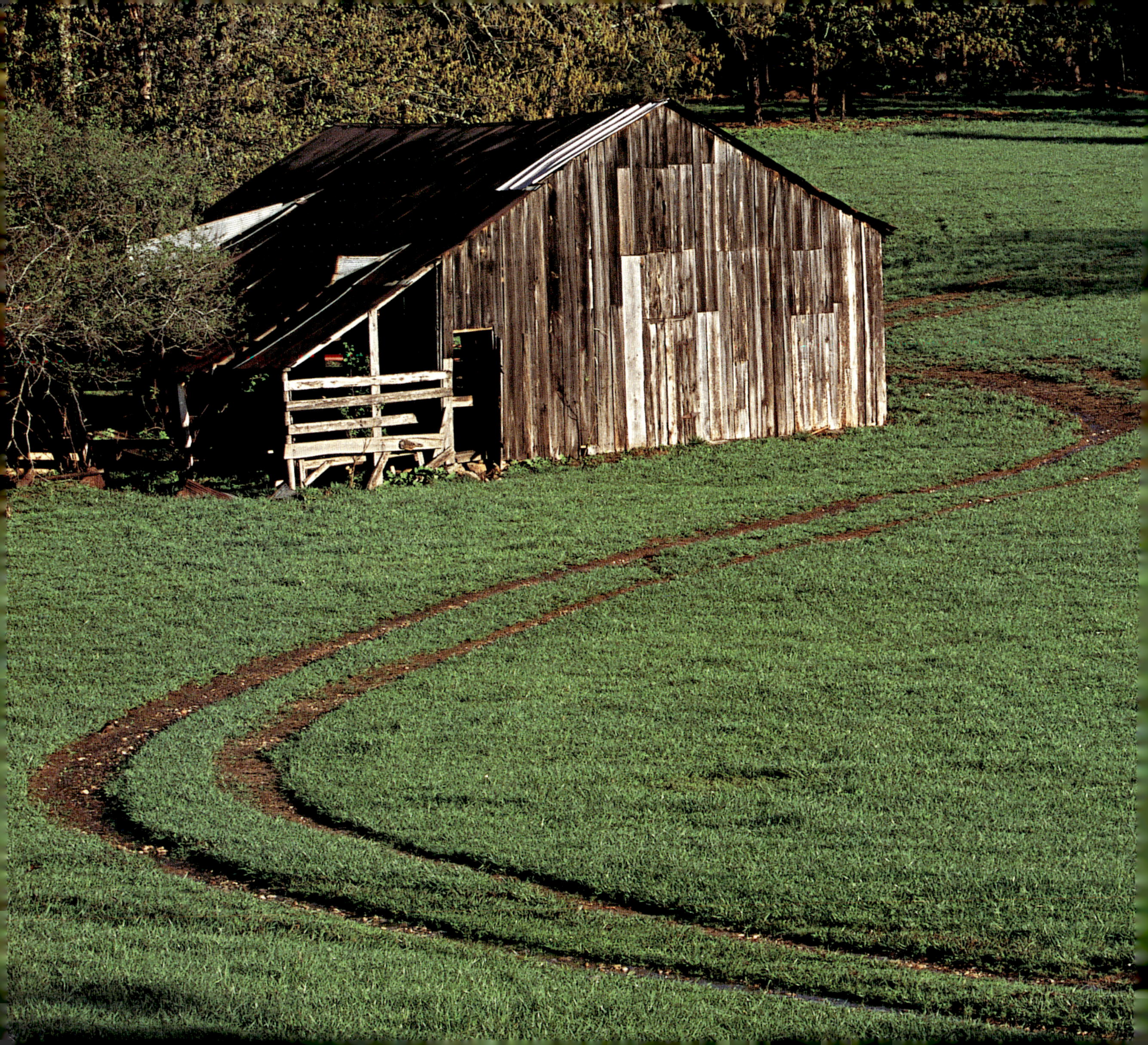

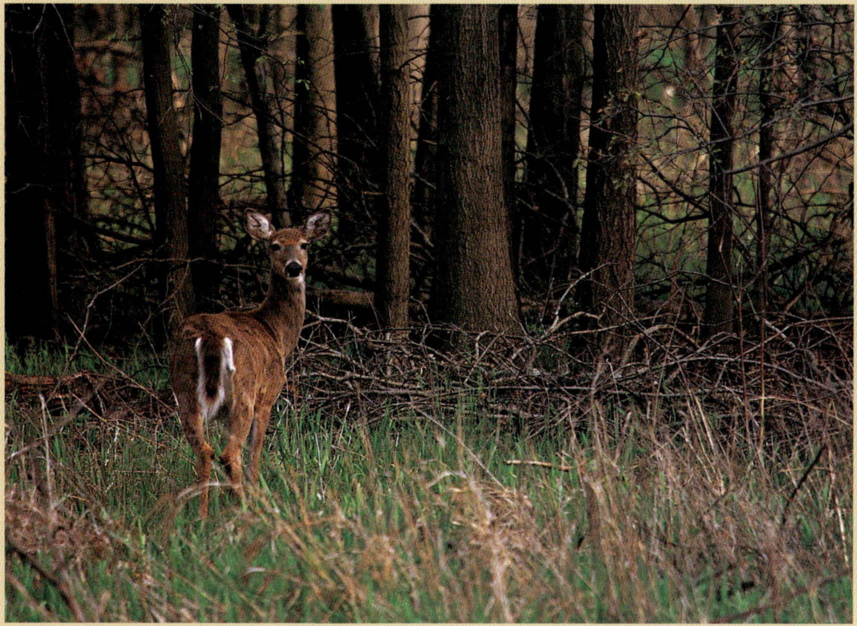

Above: This white-tailed deer at Route 66 State Park is alert and ready to flee. Missouri has successfully restored sustainable deer populations. The state manages hundreds of natural areas, conservation areas, and state parks.

Left: Weathered wood and a tin roof keep livestock and feed sheltered at a farm in Shannon County.

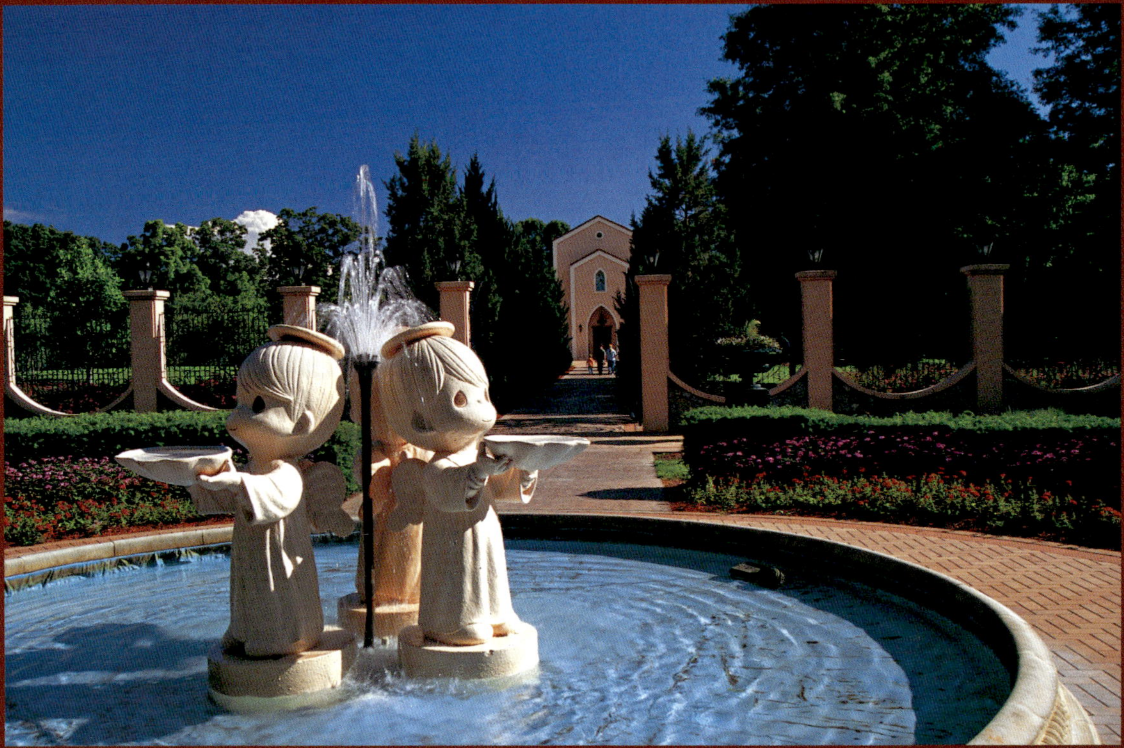

Above: The Wishing Fountain is a popular attraction at Precious Moments Park, located in Carthage. The park's chapel has nearly 5,000 square feet of murals that depict stories from the Bible.

Right: Missouri chose the eastern bluebird as its state bird. Here, at Prairie State Park, a bluebird has captured a fat insect larva for her breakfast—or perhaps she's feeding her young. Bluebirds in Missouri sometimes raise two clutches a year.

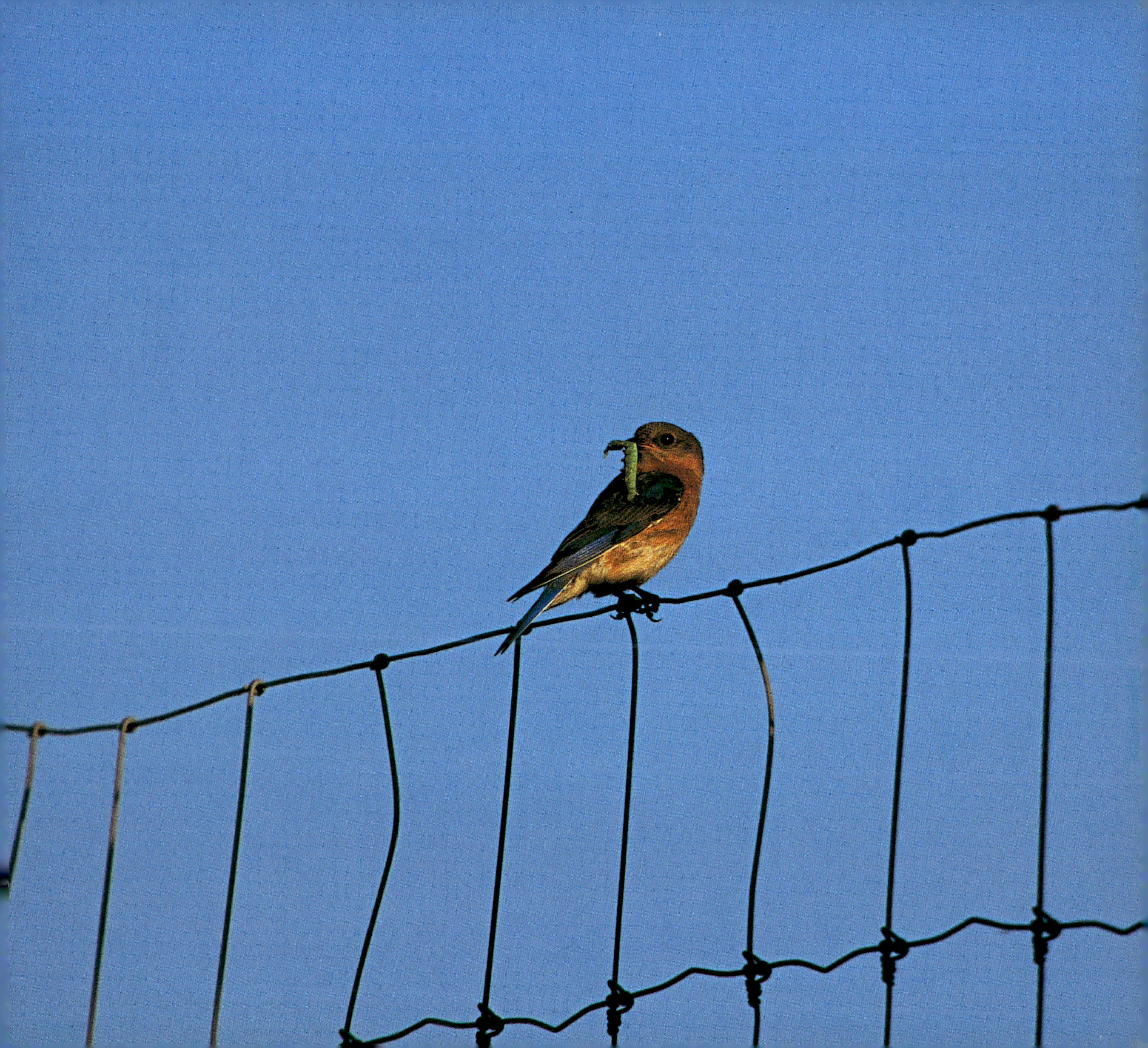

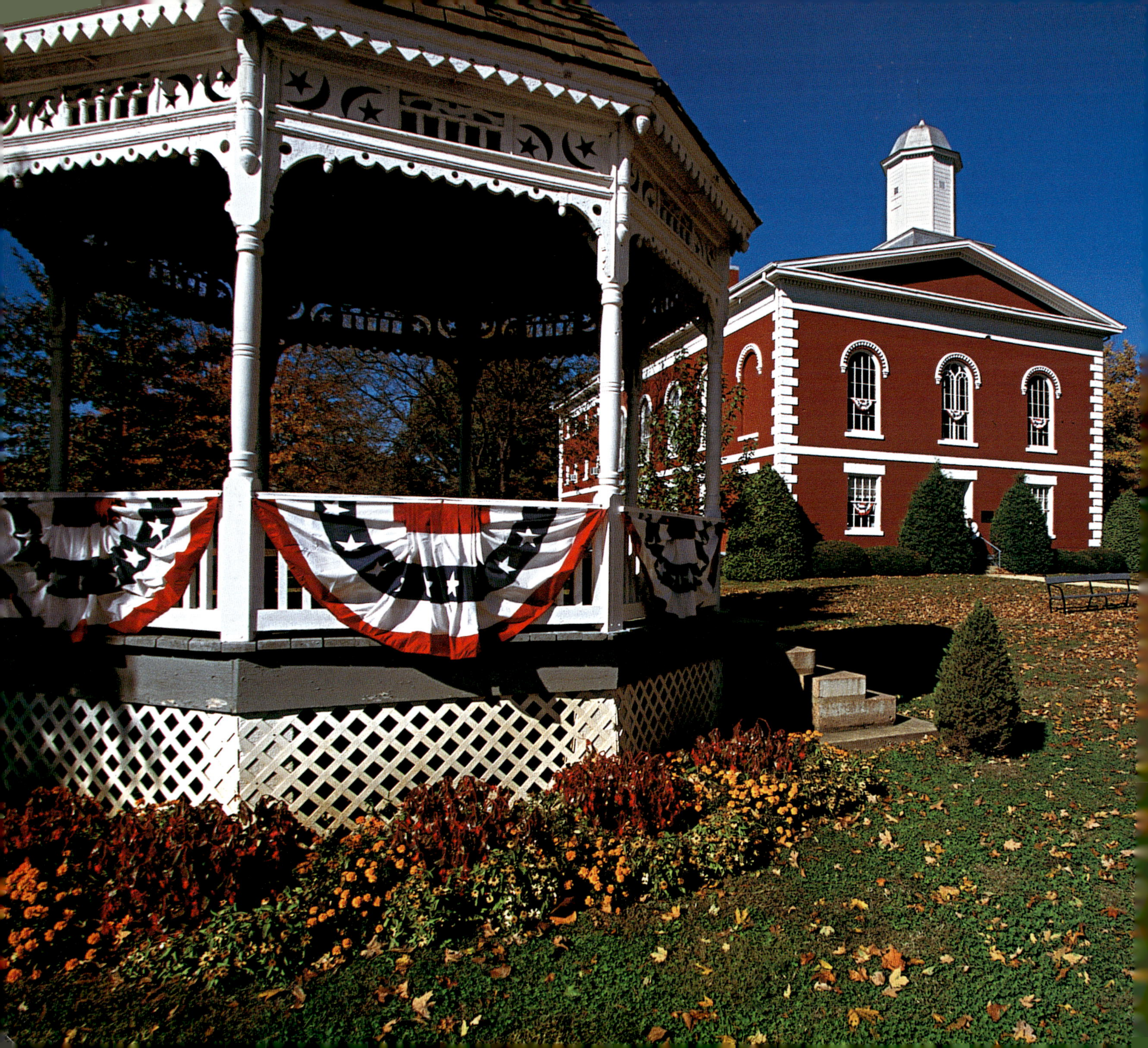

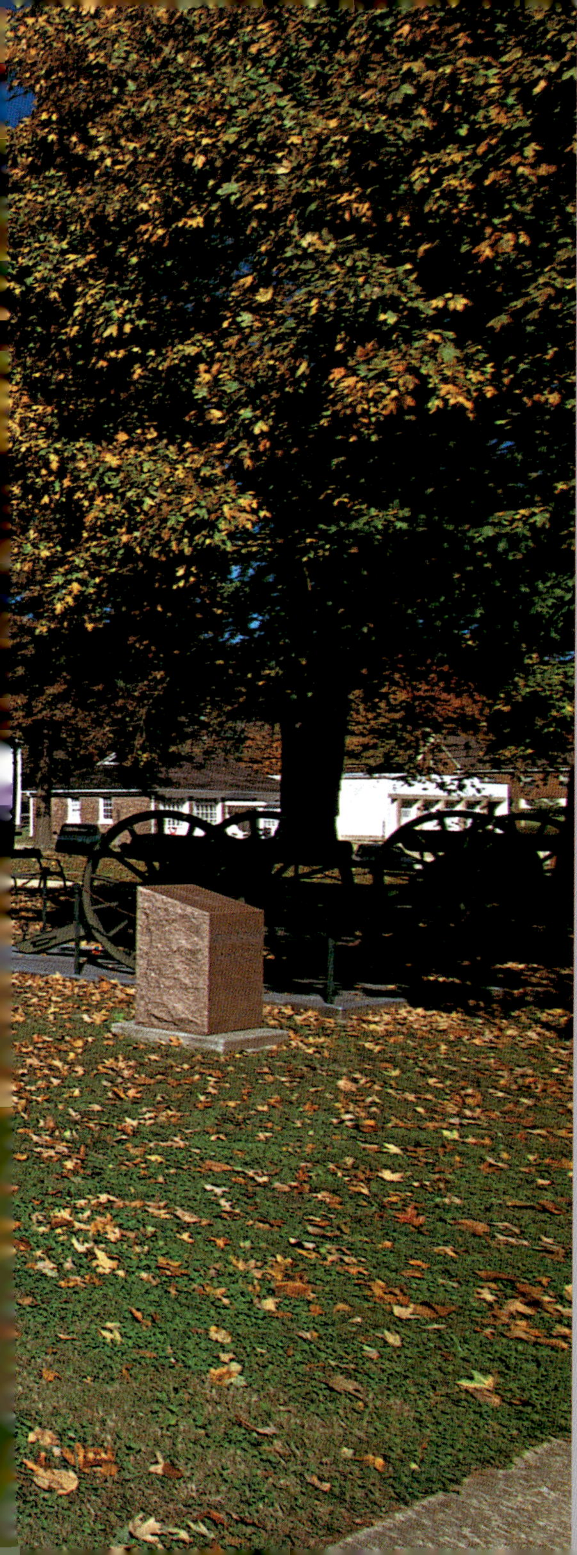

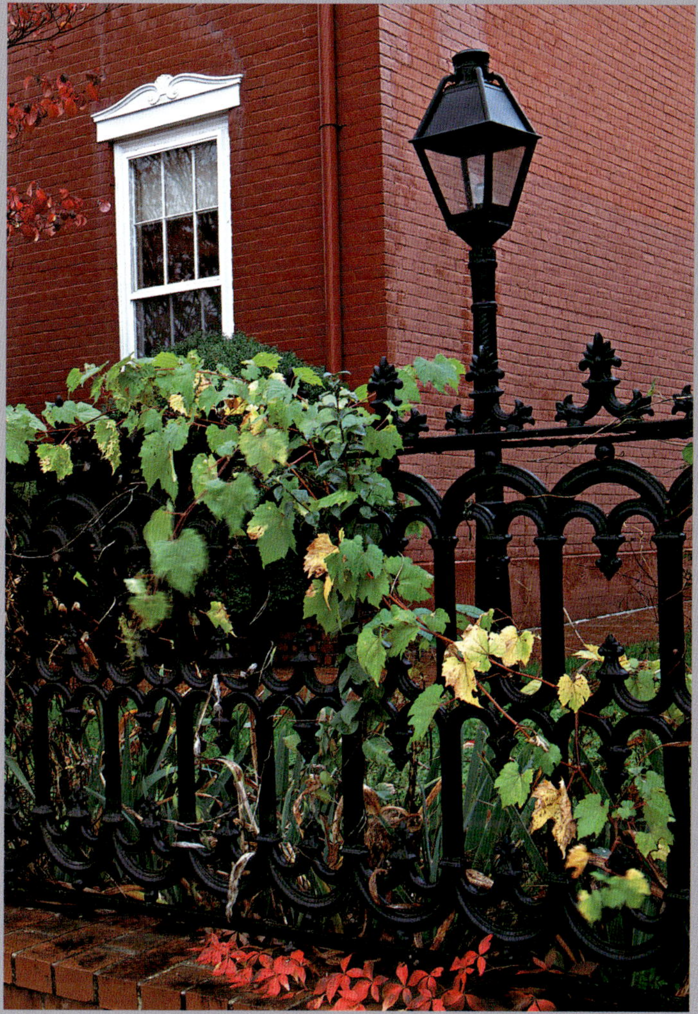

Above: The city of Hermann has more than 150 lovingly maintained historic buildings. German immigrants established this community in the middle to late nineteenth century.

Left: The gazebo is draped and ready for celebrations, in the park near the immaculately preserved City Hall in Ironton. This is the site of a Civil War battle; a scar left by a cannonball is still visible on the east face of the City Hall.

Right: Big Spring flows into the Current River, part of the Ozark National Scenic Riverways. This is the largest freshwater spring in the United States, on average pouring forth more than 270 million gallons a day from subterranean caves and tunnels.

Below: Viewers can safely get up close and personal with sharks at Wonders of Wildlife, in Springfield. Indoor and outdoor exhibits here display more than 225 species of animals in natural habitats.

PHOTO COURTESY OF WONDERS OF WILDLIFE, THE NATIONAL FISH AND WILDLIFE MUSEUM AND ZOOQUARIUM

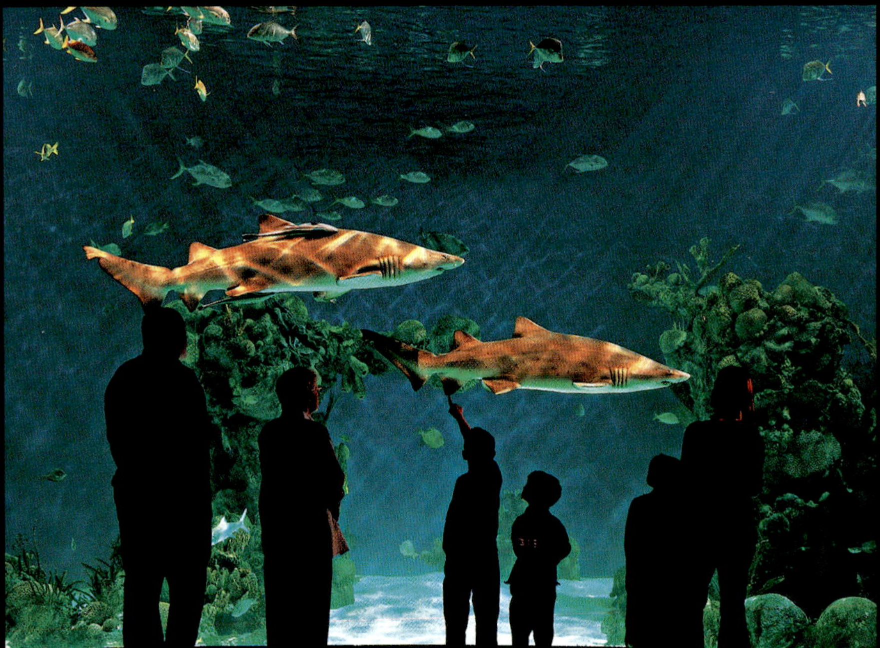

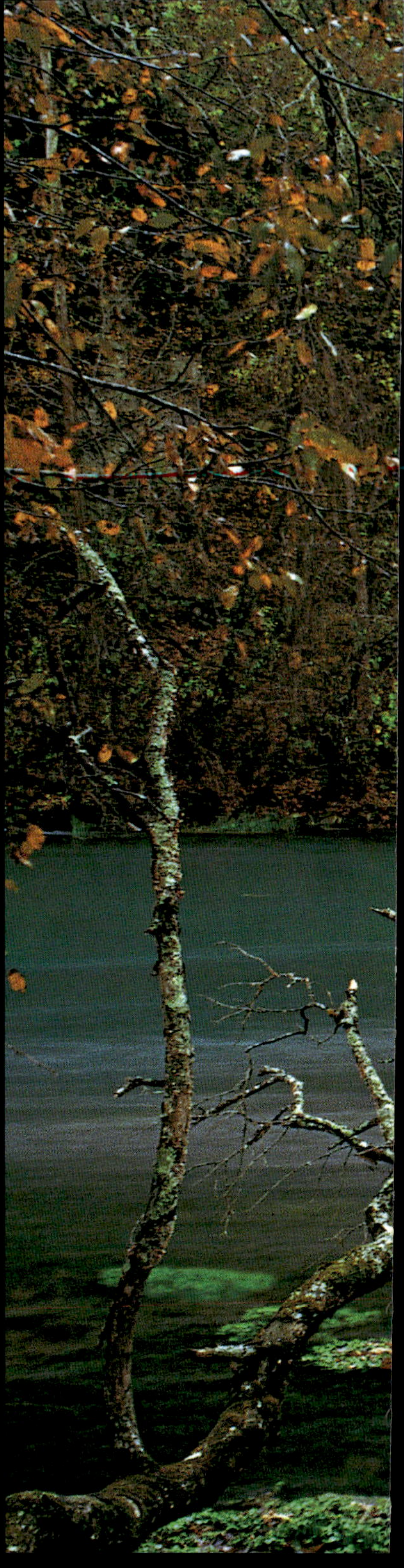

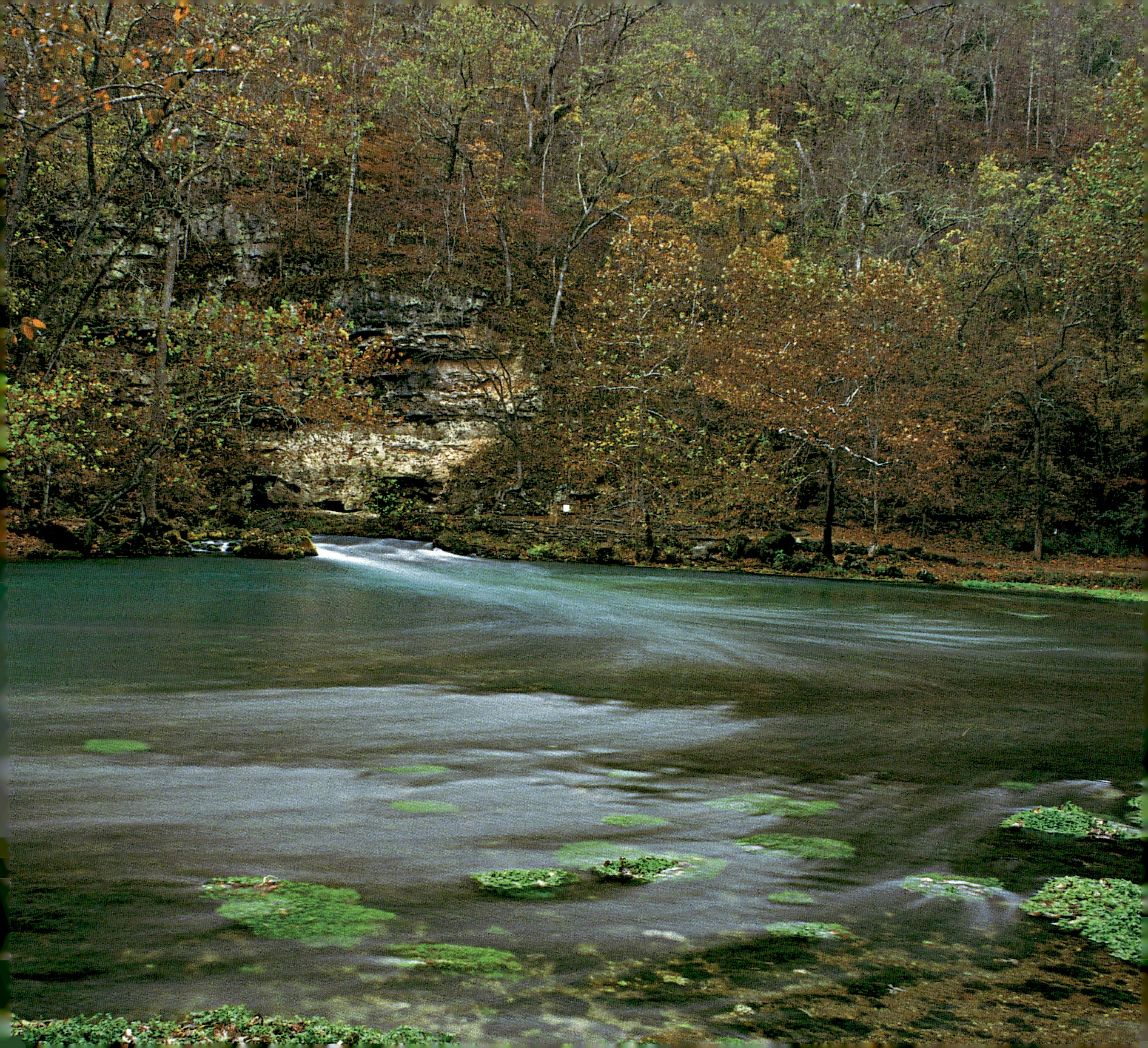

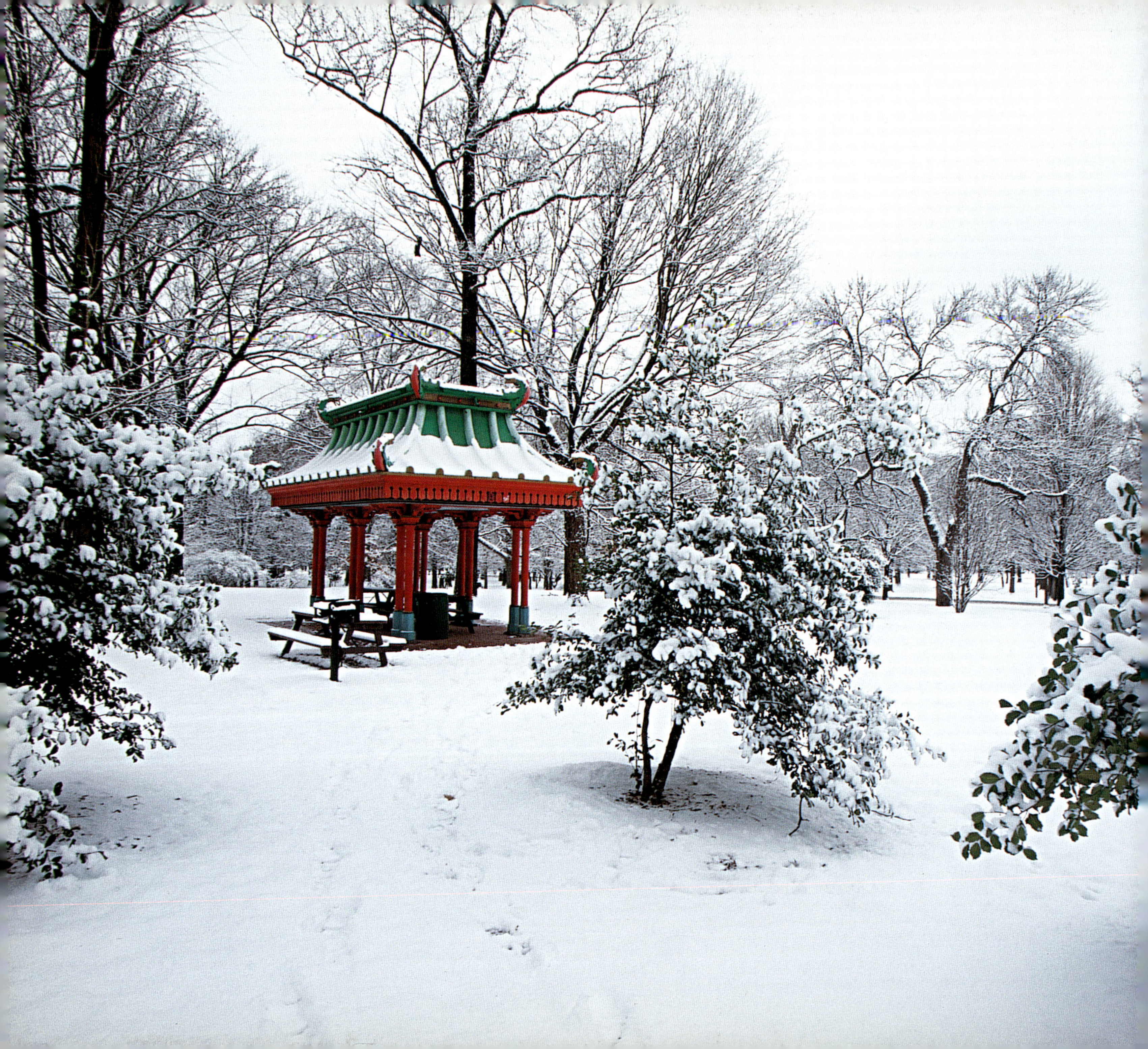

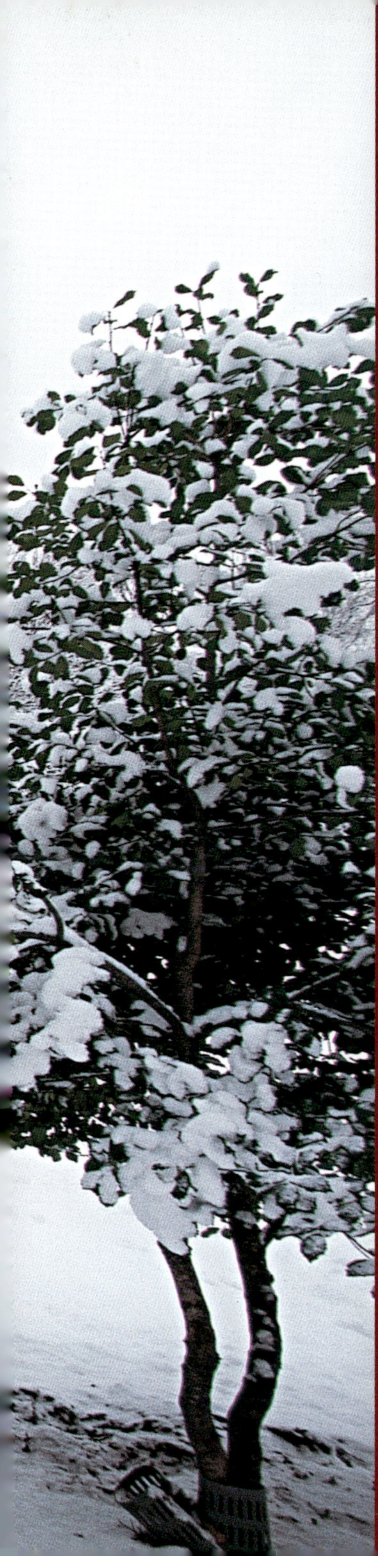

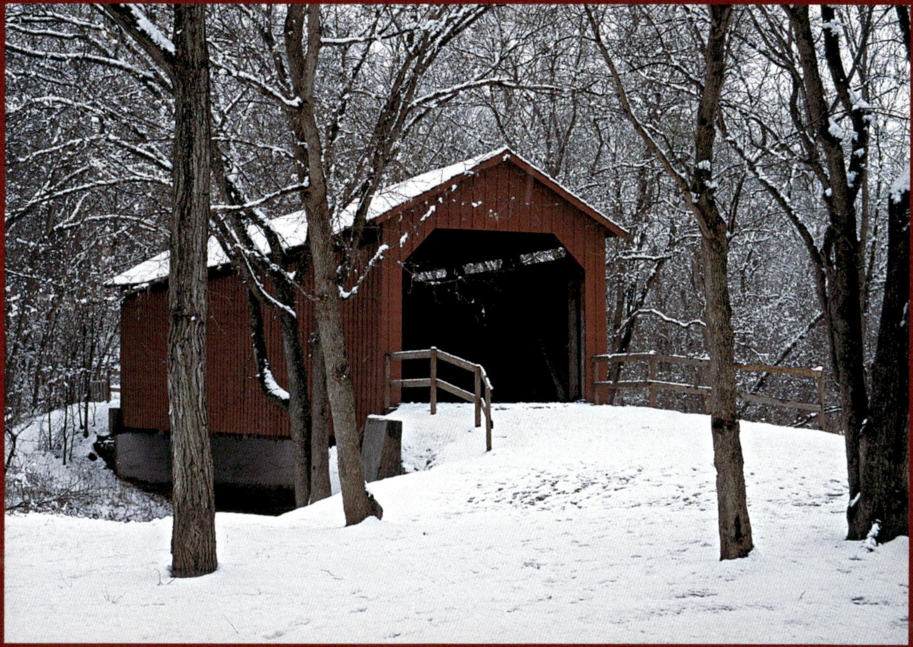

Above: This covered bridge offers a dry way across Sandy Creek, in Jefferson County. The bridge, near Hillsboro, has sheltered travelers since 1872 and is now preserved as a state historic site.

Left: Hardy picnickers in St. Louis can find a dry table year-round under this picturesque shelter at Tower Grove Park, established in 1868. Before donating the park to the city, the original owner, Henry Shaw, brought in more than 8,000 shrubs and trees from around the world.

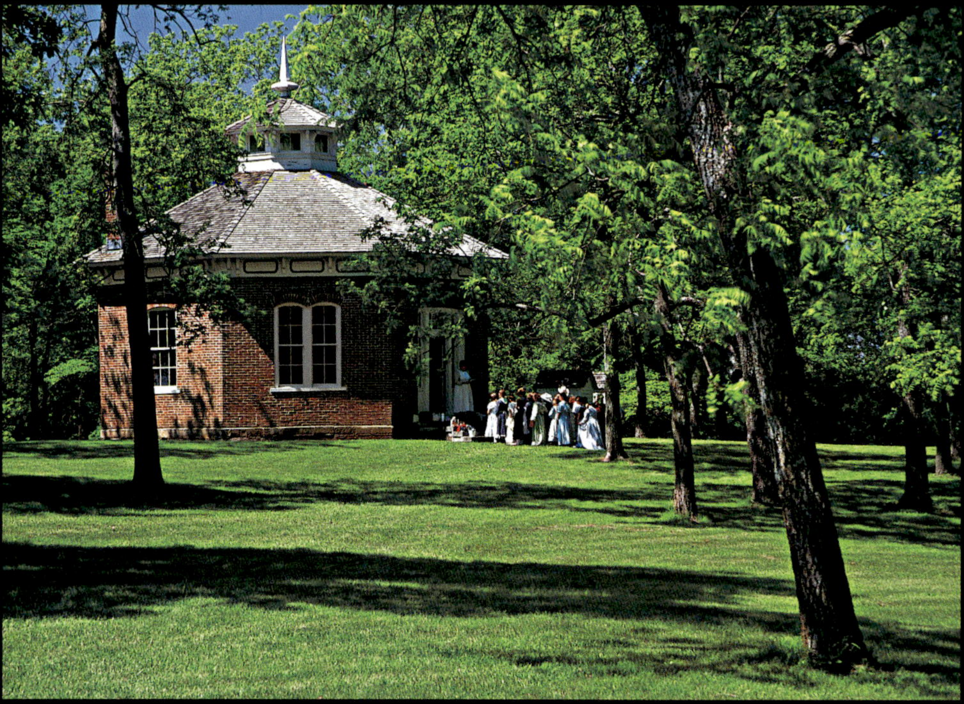

Above: Five Watkins children attended Franklin Academy in 1856. After a public school was built in the 1870s, the building was sold to Waltus Watkins and used as housing for his workers. Today it serves as part of the Living History Farm Program at Watkins Woolen Mill State Park and State Historic Site.

Right: Home of Harry S. Truman, the nation's 33rd president, Independence hosts the Truman Presidential Museum and Library. The spacious building features exhibits on his presidency as well as his pre- and post-presidency life, plus artifacts and other displays.

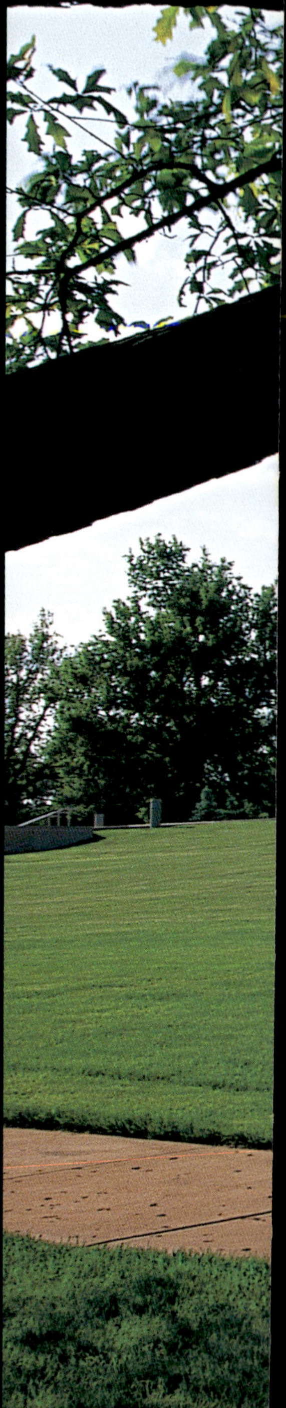

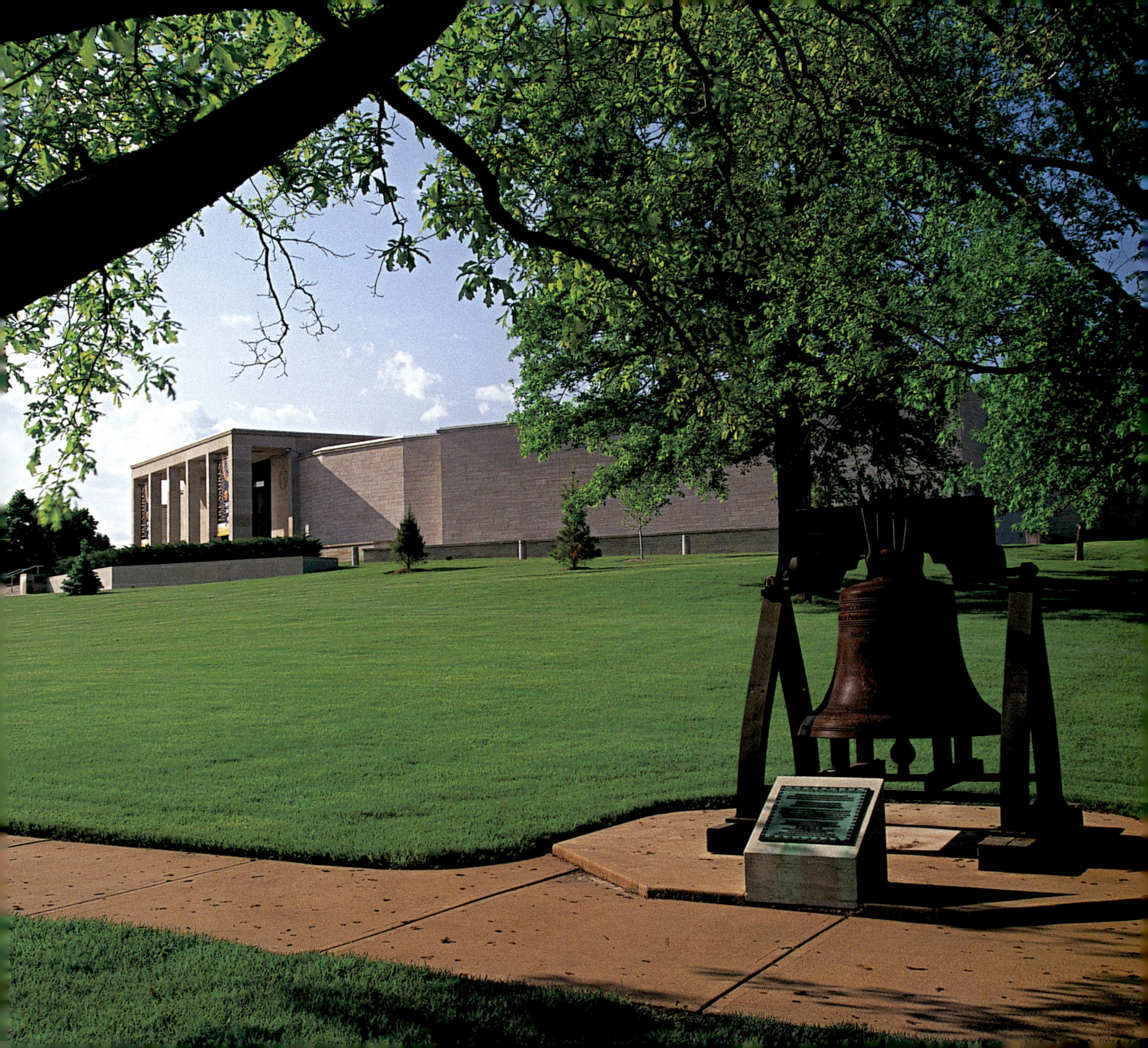

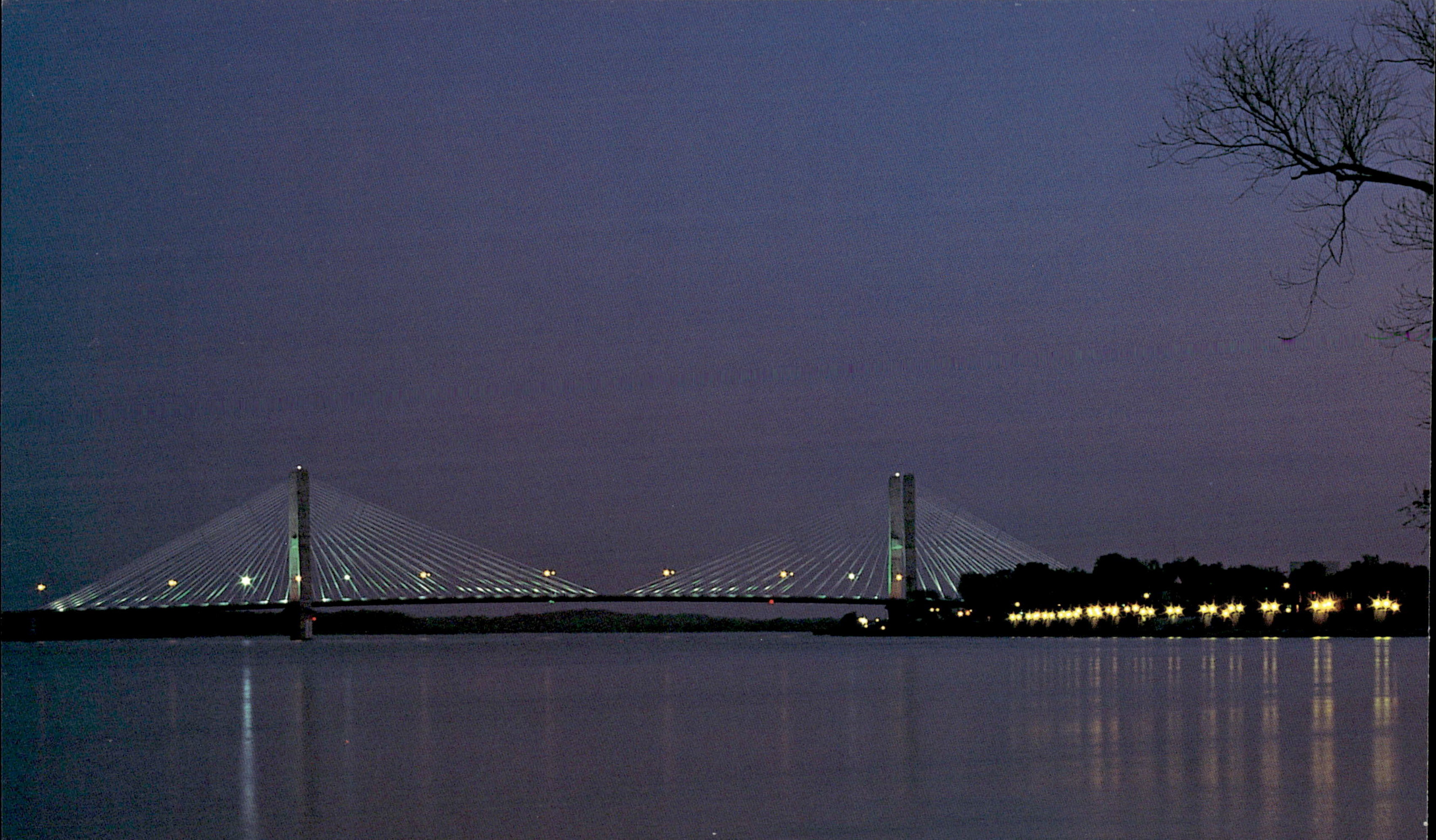

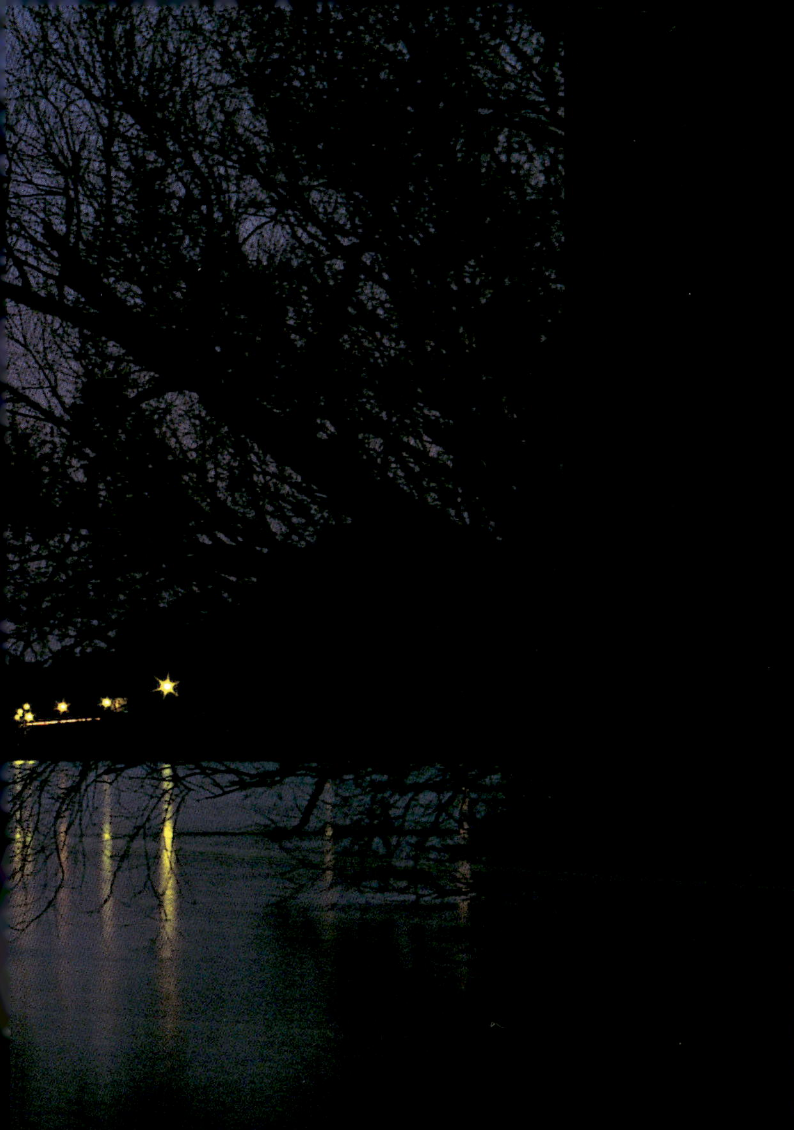

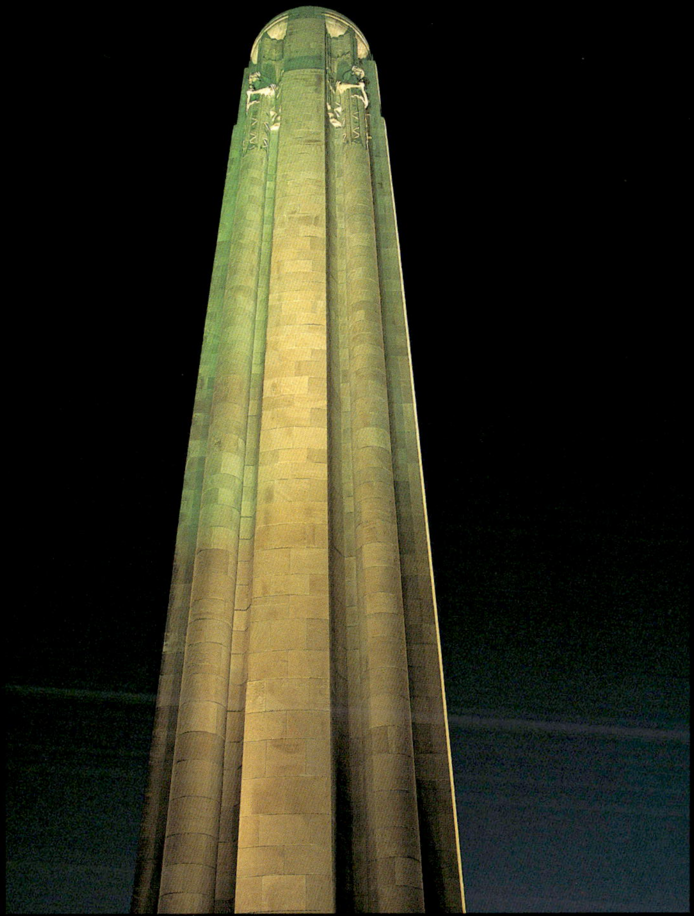

Above: The 217-foot Memorial Tower is an unmistakable feature of the Liberty Memorial, built in Kansas City in 1926 and is now a national historic landmark. Displays include the highly interactive National World War I Museum.

Left: The Emerson Memorial Bridge spans the Mississippi River, connecting Missouri's Cape Girardeau to East Cape Girardeau in Illinois. The elegant design used 171 miles of cable, 13 million pounds of reinforcing steel, and more than 243 million pounds of concrete.

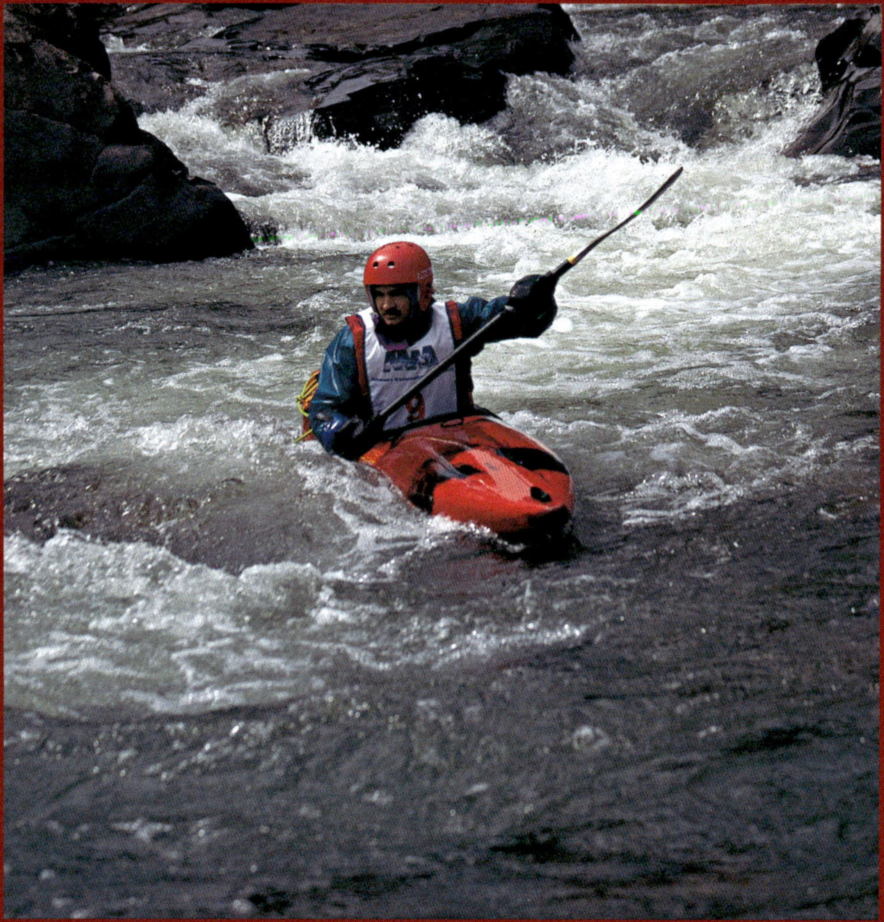

Above: A whitewater kayaker finds plenty of room to play in the Castor River's currents and eddies.

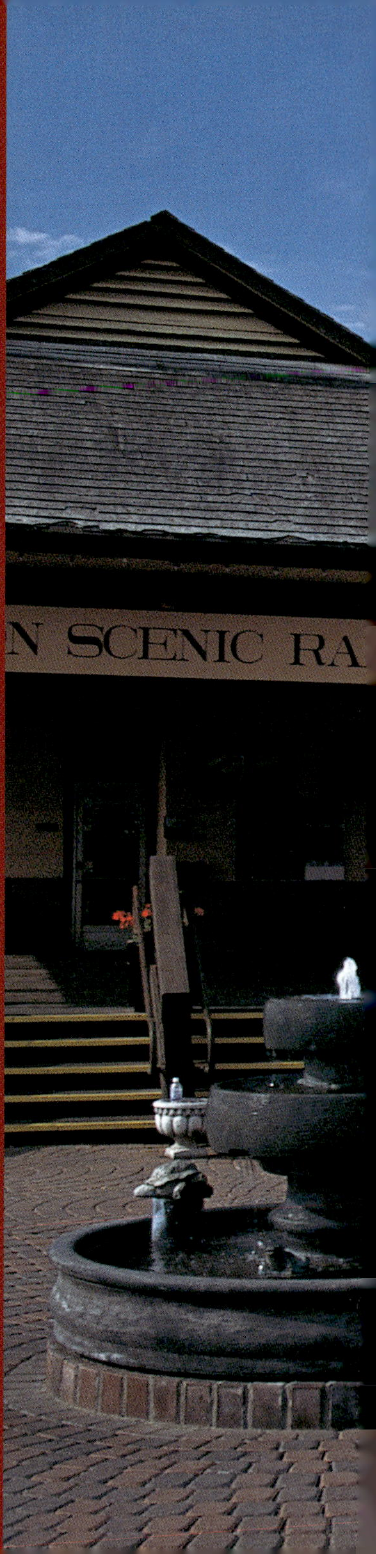

Right: The Branson Scenic Railway takes visitors on a 40-mile tour through tunnels and over trestles in the hilly Ozarks that surround this busy tourist town. Excursions leave from the depot, built in 1905.

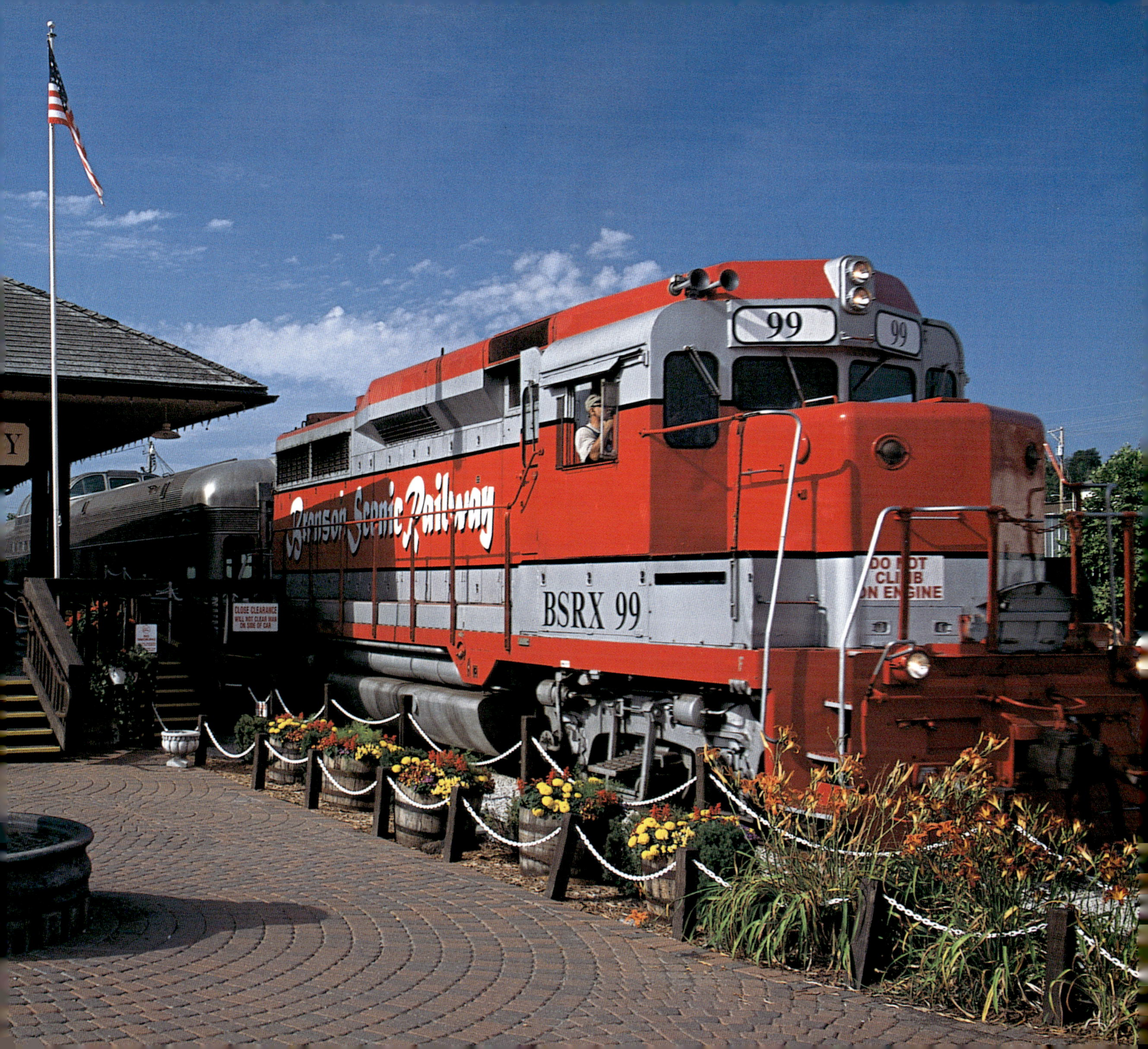
99
99
Branson Scenic Railway
BSRX 99

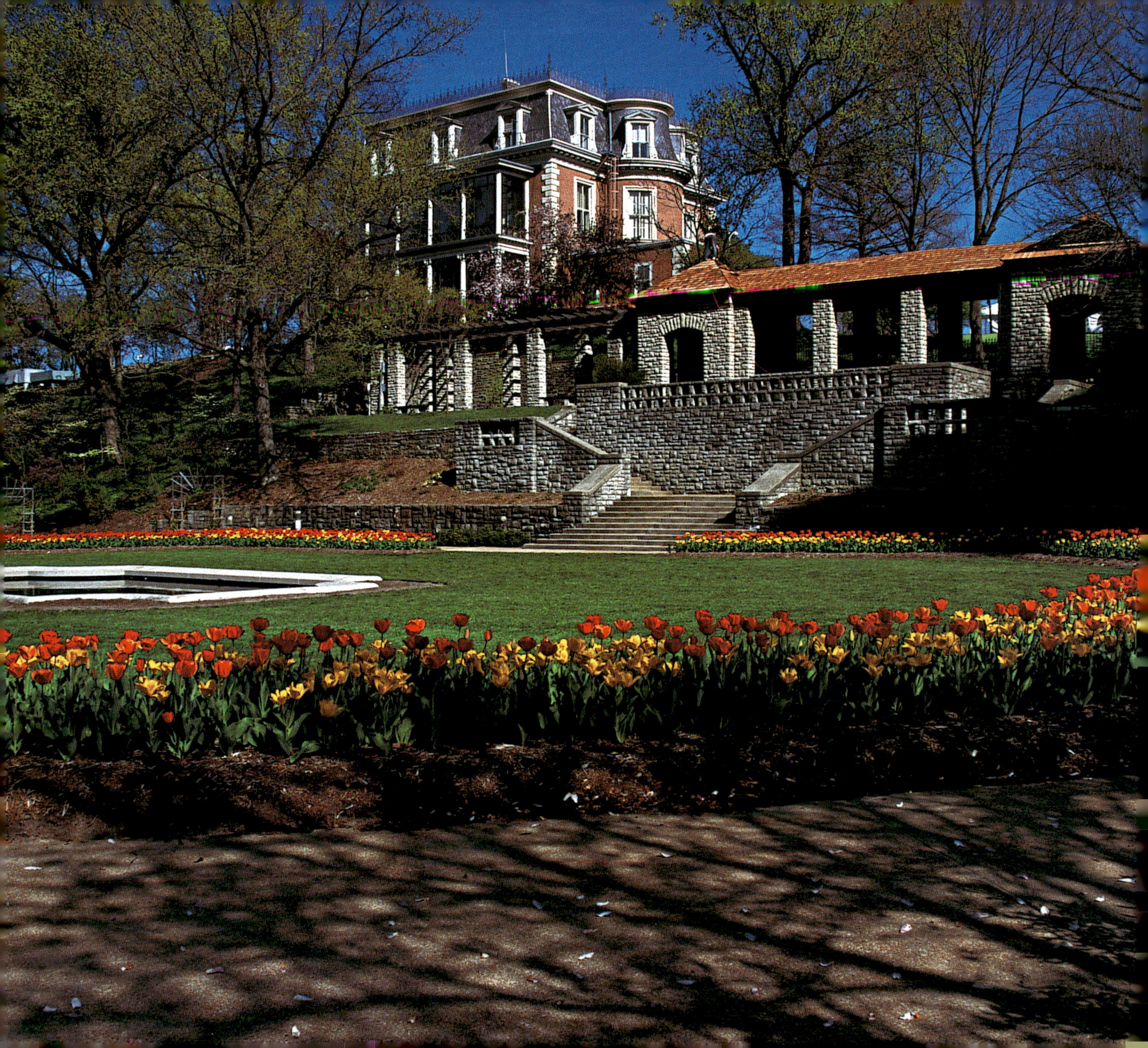

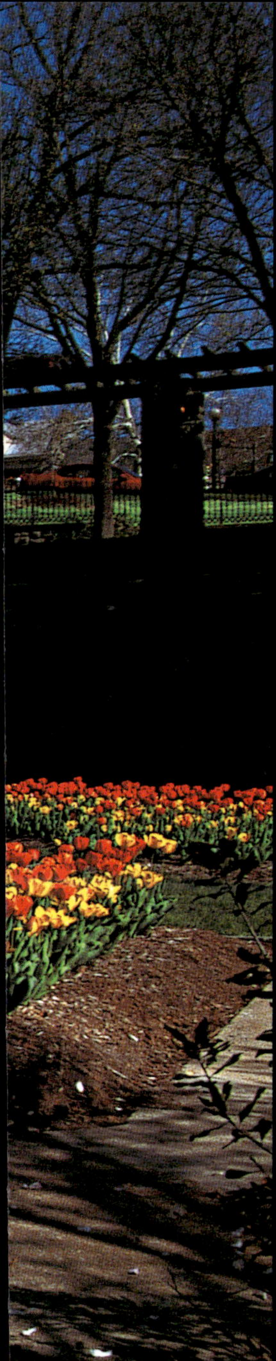

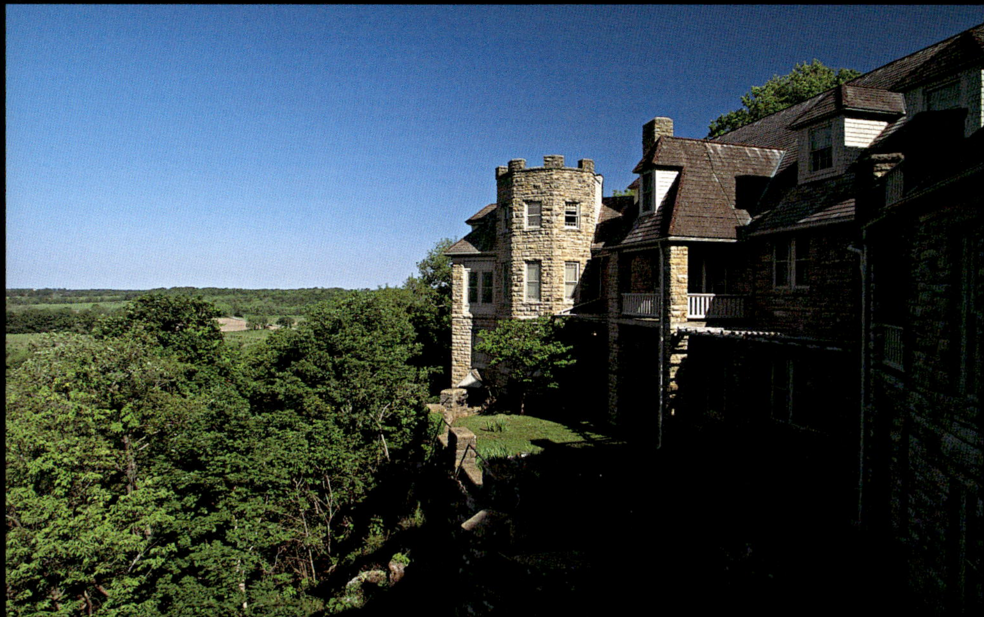

Above: The 31-room, 12,000-square-foot Bothwell Lodge was built atop natural caves north of Sedalia at the turn of the century. It is now preserved as a state historic site.

Left: Spring's dazzling display of tulips competes for your attention with the intricate stonework on the grounds of the governor's mansion. Jefferson City, near the geographic center of the state, was selected as the state capital in 1821.

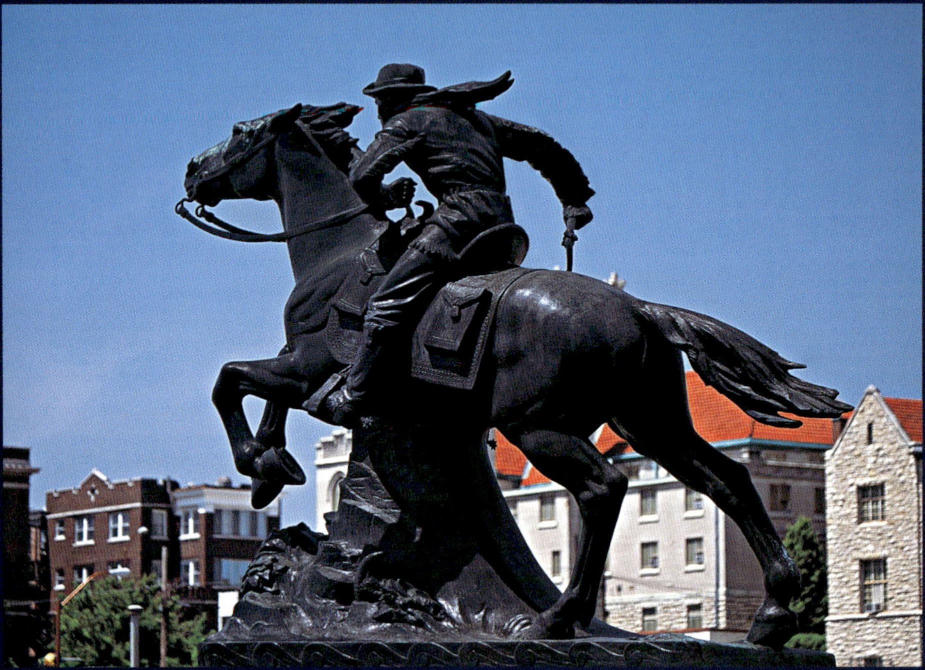

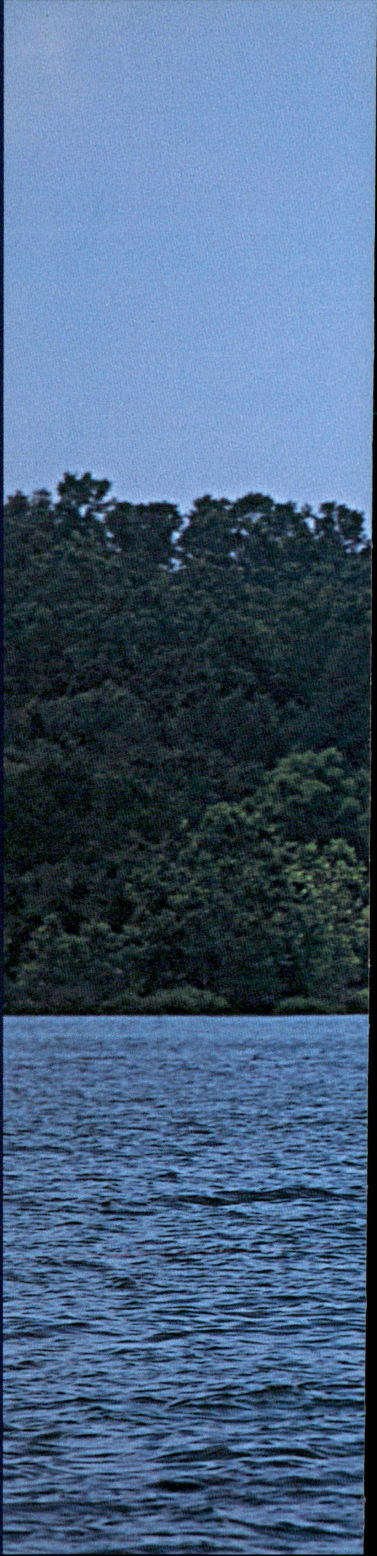

Above: St. Joseph is home to the Pony Express Museum. A statue of a galloping horse and rider commemorates this brief, romanticized era of settling America's frontier. In 1860–61, teams of relay riders carried mail across a 2,000-mile route from St. Joseph to Sacramento, California.

Right: The *Branson Belle* paddle wheeler plies the waters of scenic Table Rock Lake. Guests can enjoy sumptuous dining while professional singers and dancers provide entertainment on this showboat.

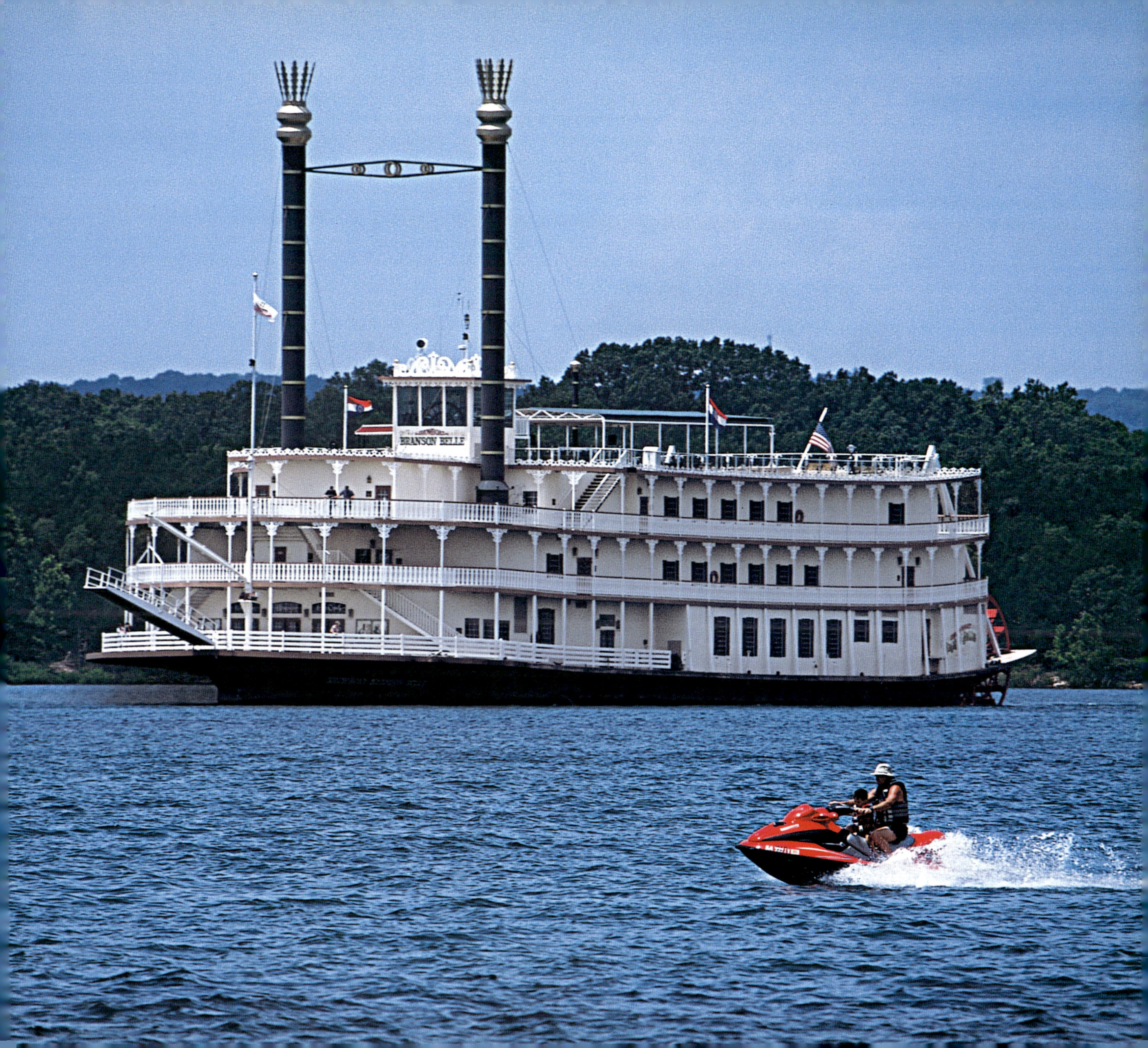
BRANSON BELLE

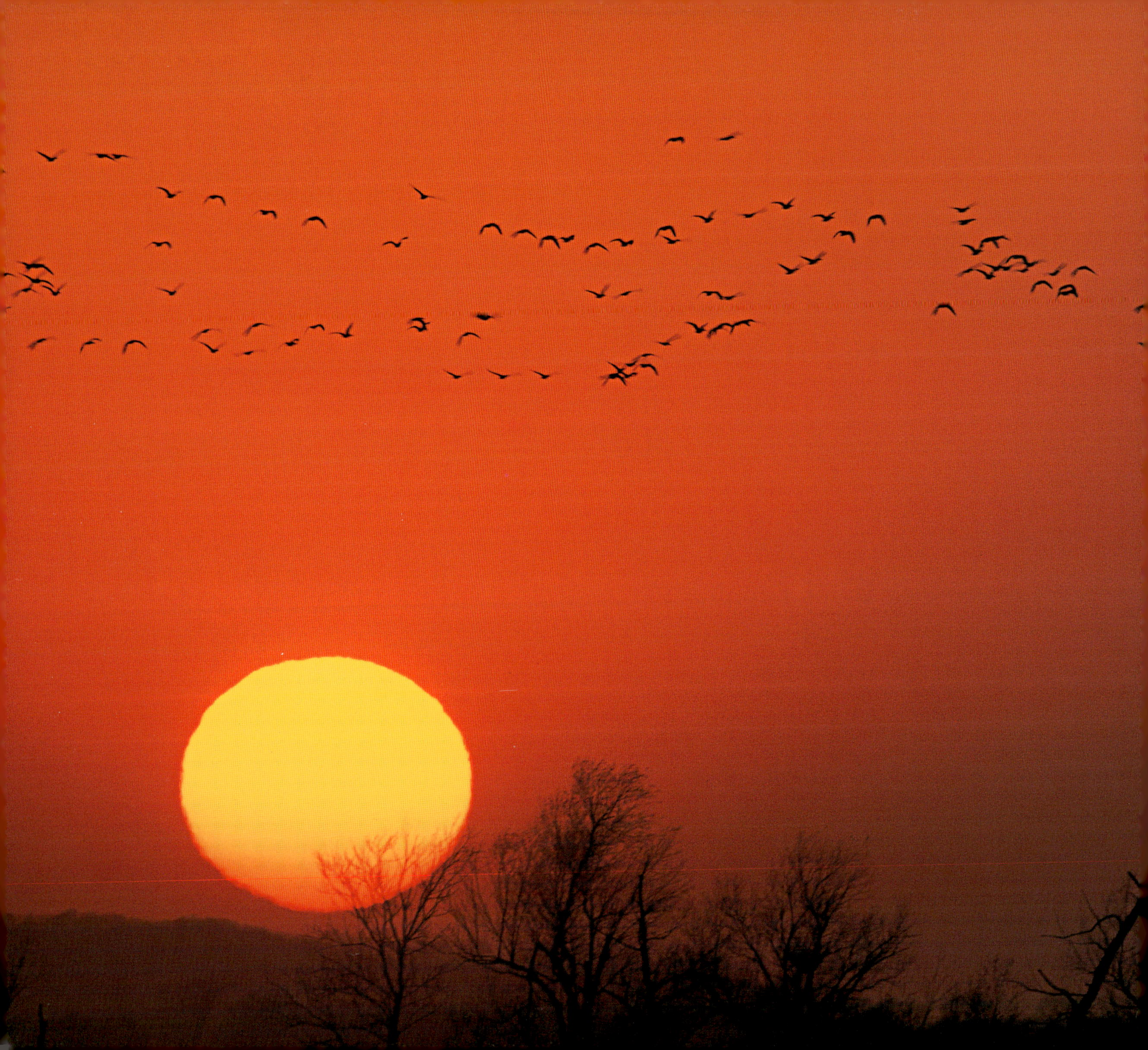

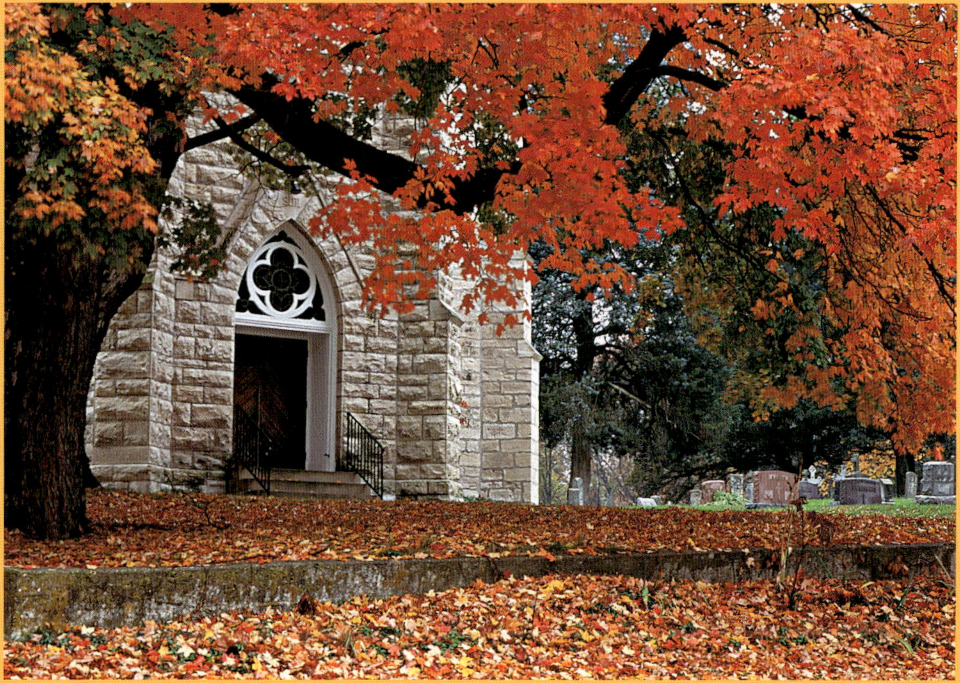

Above: A glorious display of autumn leaves frames the entrance to St. Martins of Tours Church, built in 1875 in Montgomery County.

Left: The Squaw Creek National Wildlife Refuge, established in 1935, protects 7,350 acres of wetlands, grasslands, forest, and other critical habitat in the Missouri River floodplain in northwest Missouri.

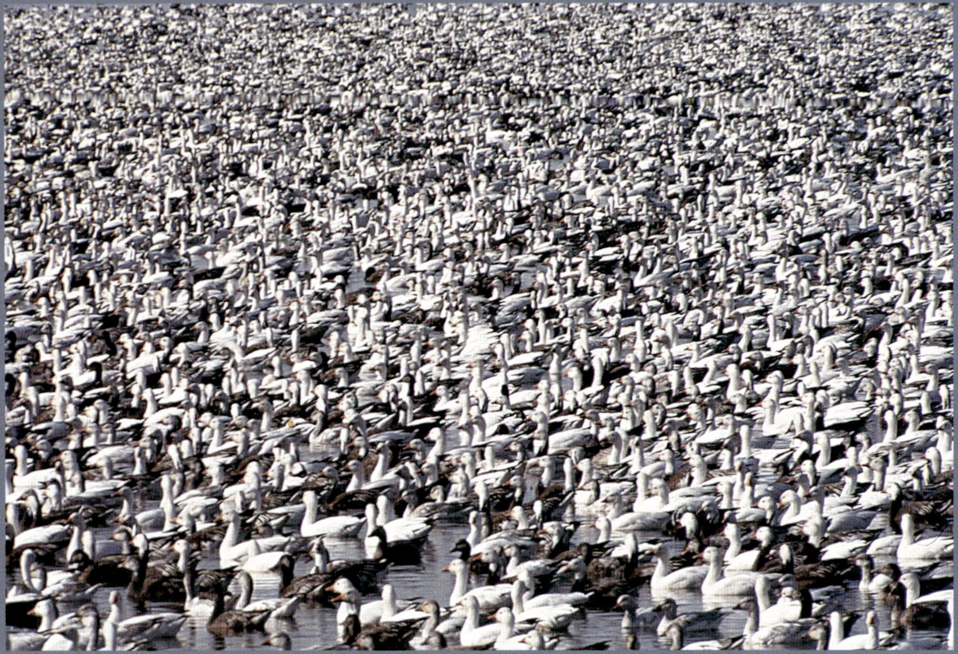

Above: Snow geese depend on the Squaw Creek National Wildlife Refuge during their spring and fall migration. About 300 species of birds are known to use the refuge, as well as 35 species of reptiles and amphibians, and 33 species of mammals.

Right: Jefferson Barracks was established in 1826 to train infantry, and it remained an active U.S. Army post until 1946. Today's visitors to St. Louis can take a guided tour of this historic park, enjoy the picnic facilities, and view the museum exhibits.

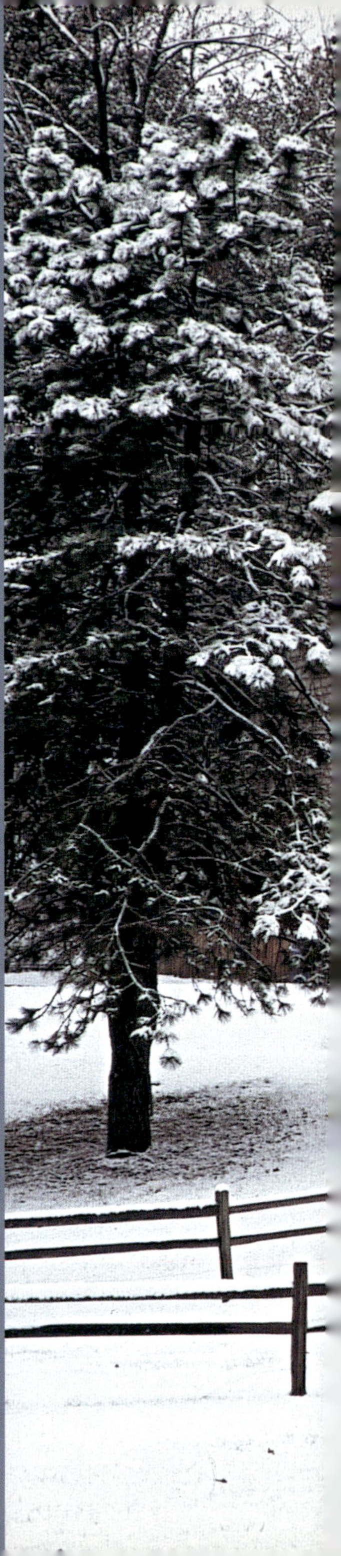

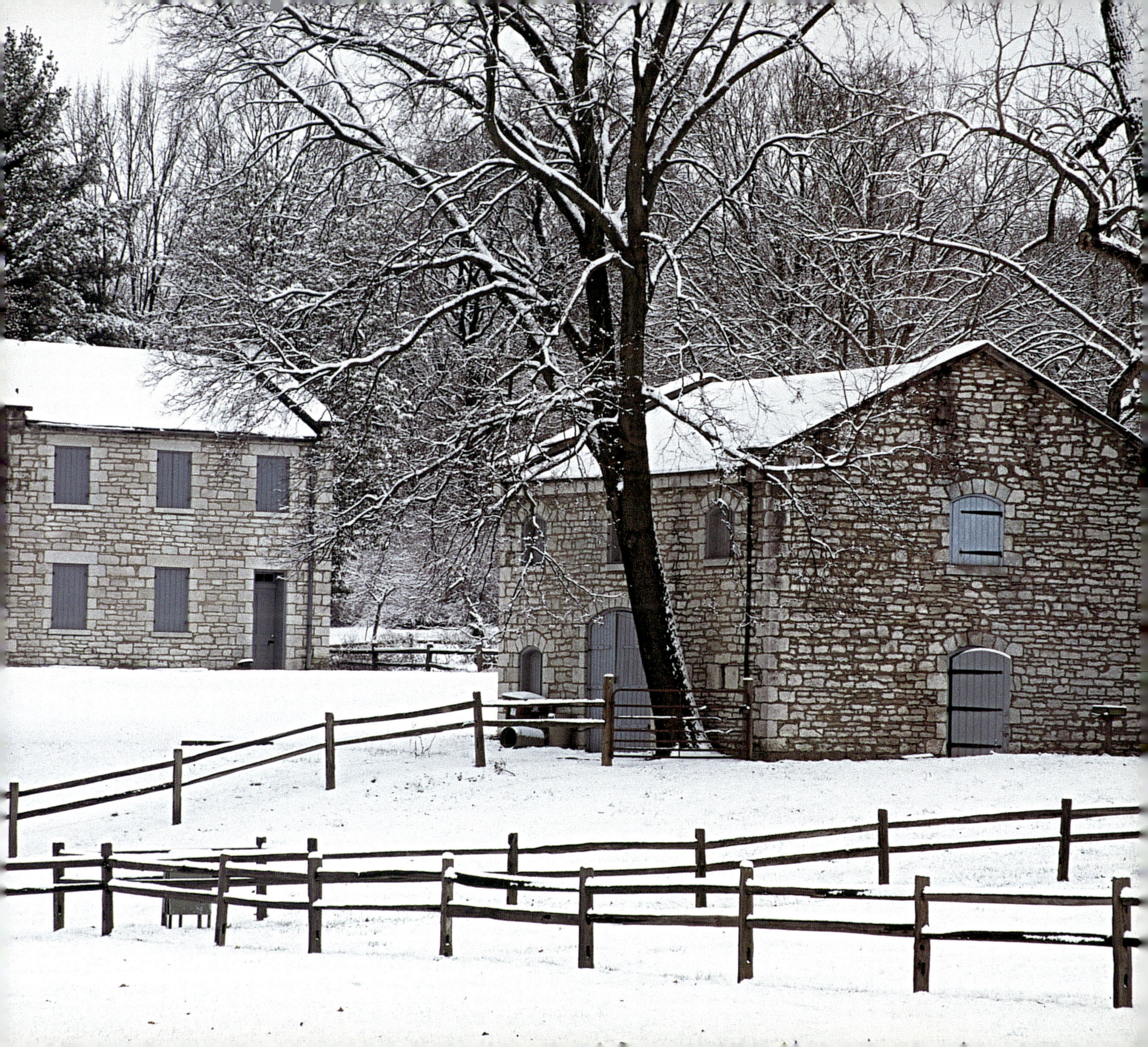

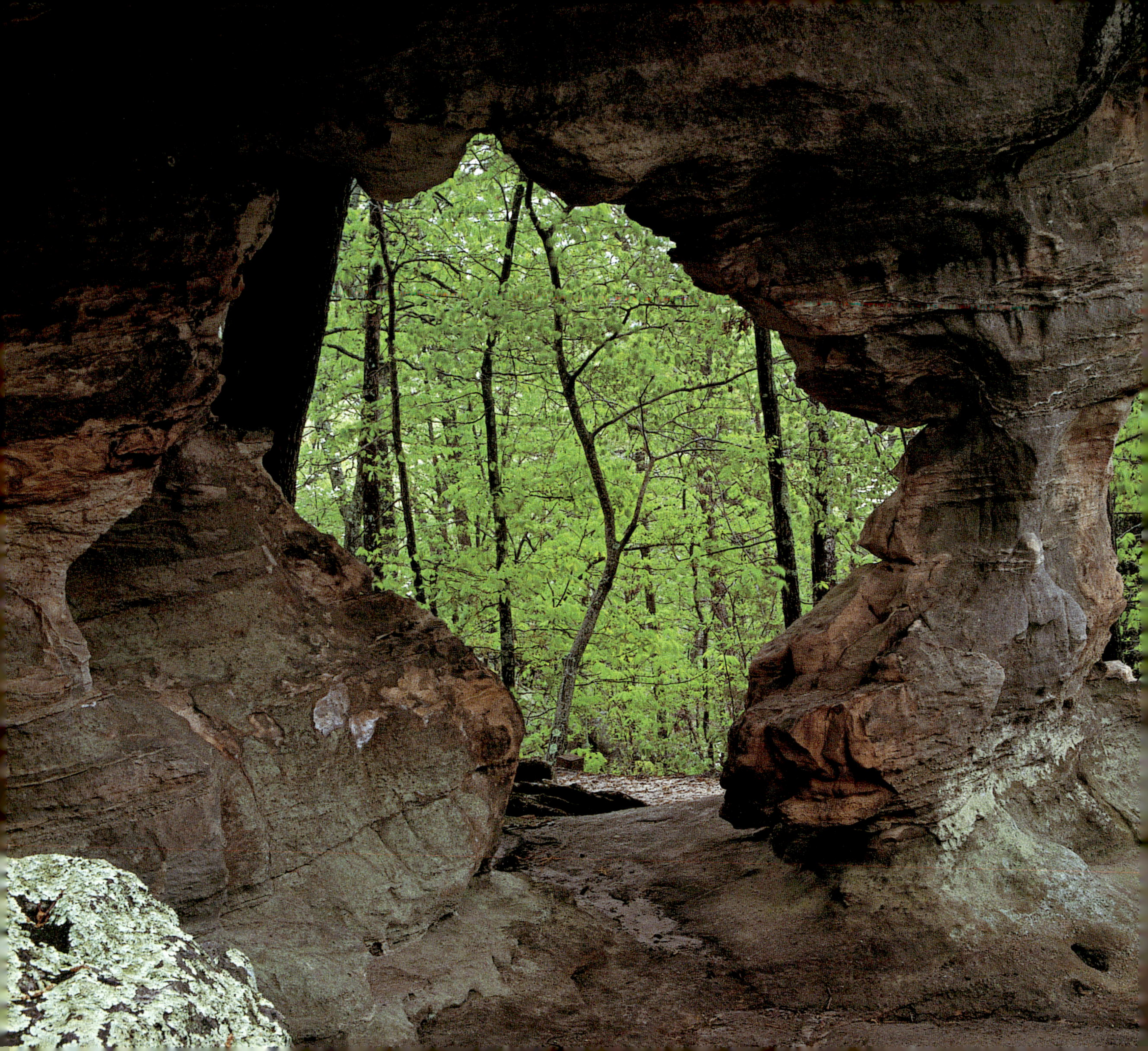

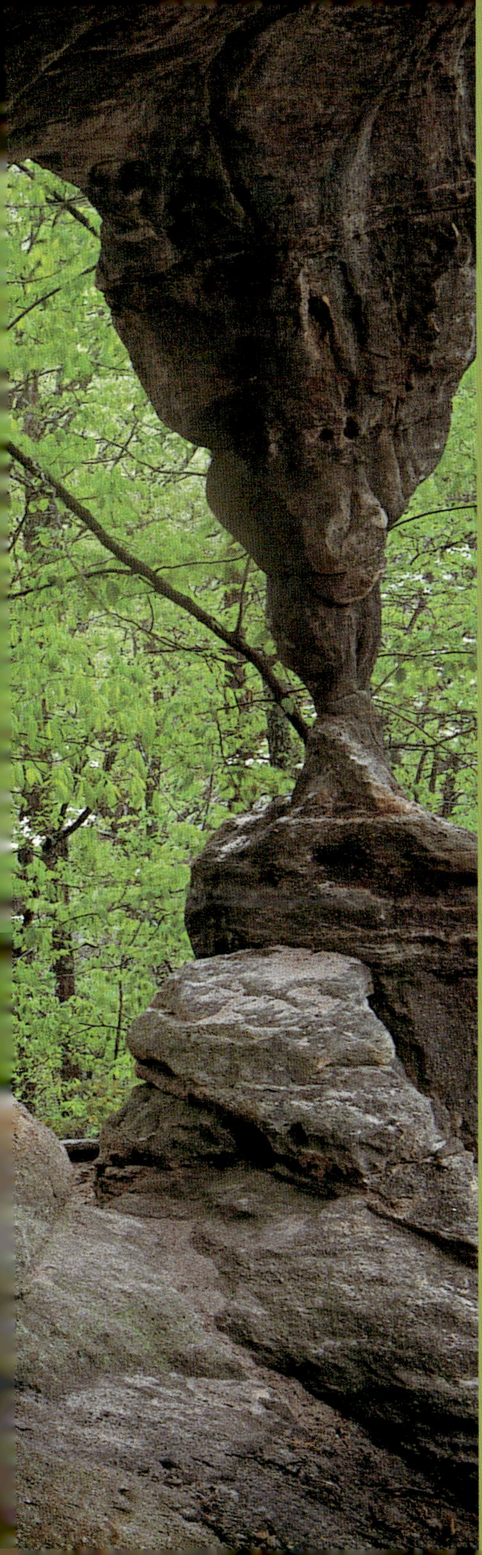

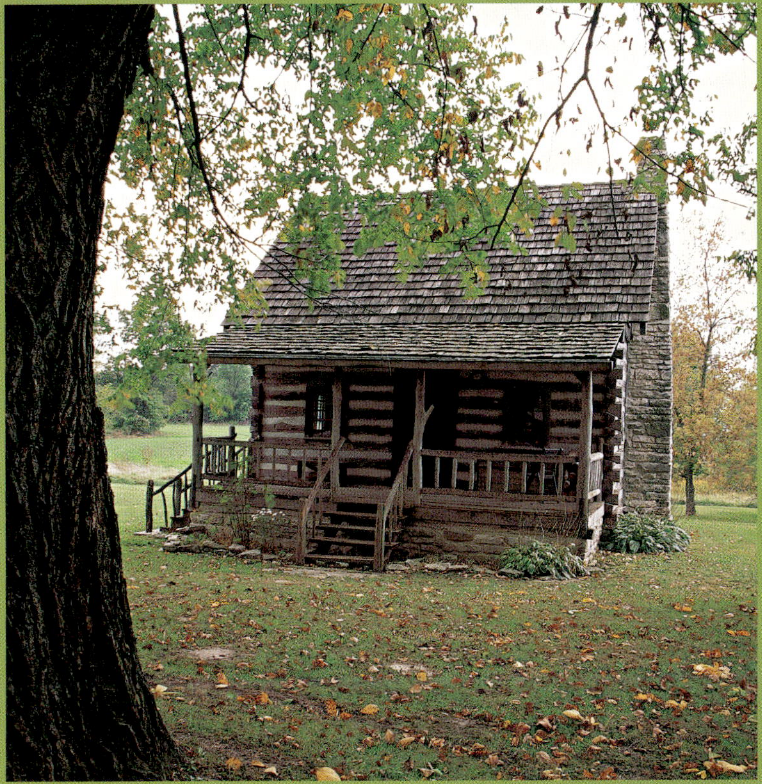

Above: Bethel residents have preserved the colony's rich German heritage, such as this log cabin. Founded in 1844 by Dr. Wilhelm Keil, this Christian community lived communally and shared the work as well as the harvest. By 1855, Bethel had 650 residents. Keil went to Oregon in 1855 with 75 followers and founded another community, which he named Aurora.

Left: The sandstone Double Arch is a prominent feature at Pickle Springs Natural Area. The two-mile "Trail Through Time" interpretive path leads through this 256-acre natural landmark that preserves fascinating geological and biological wonders.

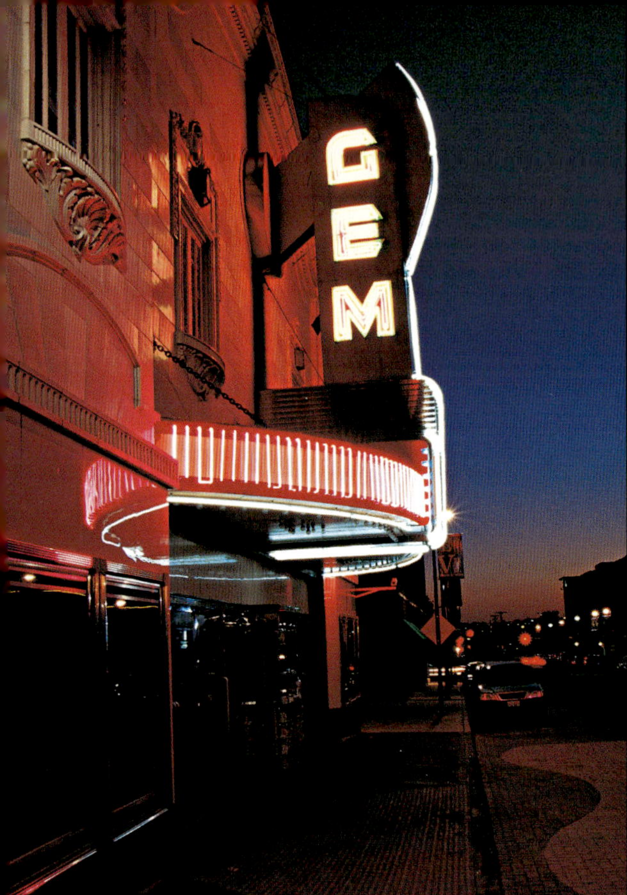

Kansas City's famous jazz district lights up at night, seen here at 18th and Vine. The unique strains of KC jazz have been heard continuously since the 1920s.

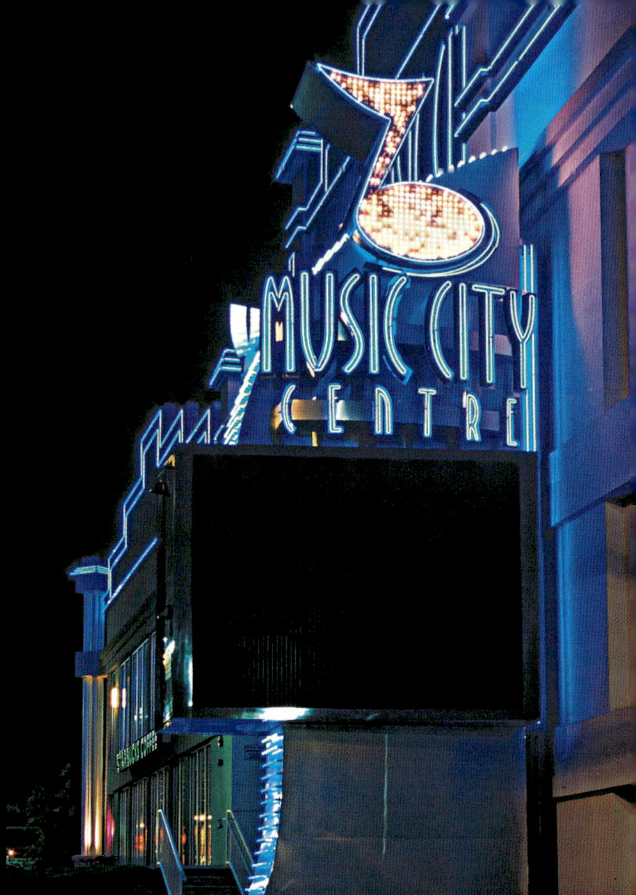

Branson has carved a unique niche for entertainment, attracting busloads of music lovers year-round. Music City Centre offers live entertainment daily.

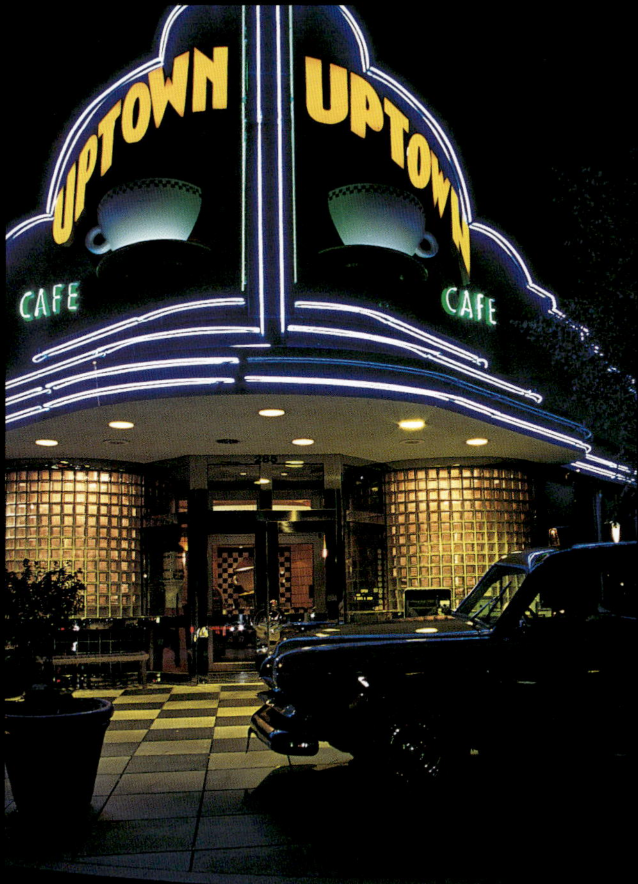

The Uptown Cafe in Branson preserves the art deco theme so representative of the 1950s, complete with neon, jukebox music, and authentic cuisine.

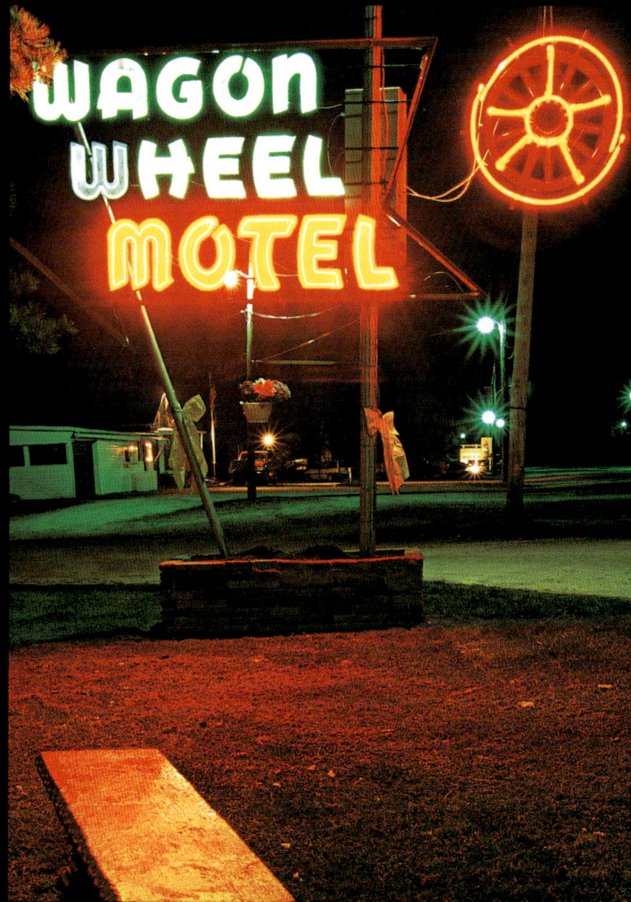

Where else would you find such a classic style of neon signage but on Route 66? This motel is in Cuba, in east-central Missouri.

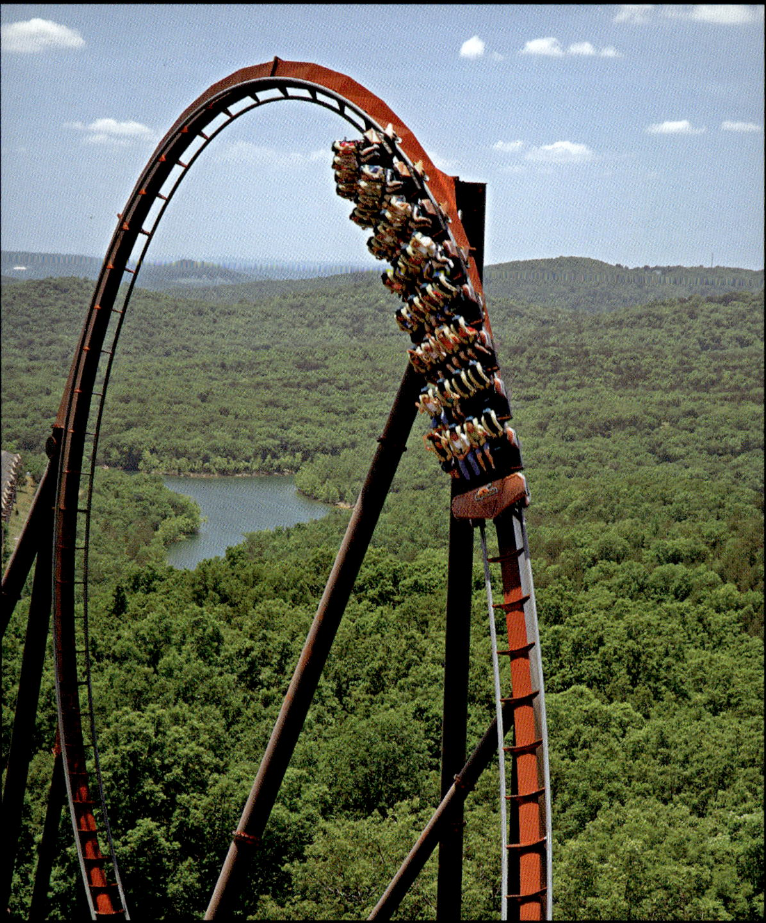

Above: They're strapped in and screamin' around the loop, on the roller coaster at Silver Dollar City Amusement Park in Branson.

PHOTO COURTESY OF HERSCHEND FAMILY ENTERTAINMENT CORPORATION, BRANSON, MISSOURI

Right: The fresh waters of this creek turned the wheel that powered Hodgson Mill's giant red granite stone, beginning in 1882. The present-day Hodgson Mill company in nearby Gainesville is known throughout the nation for grinding whole, natural grains into delicious flours and cornmeal.

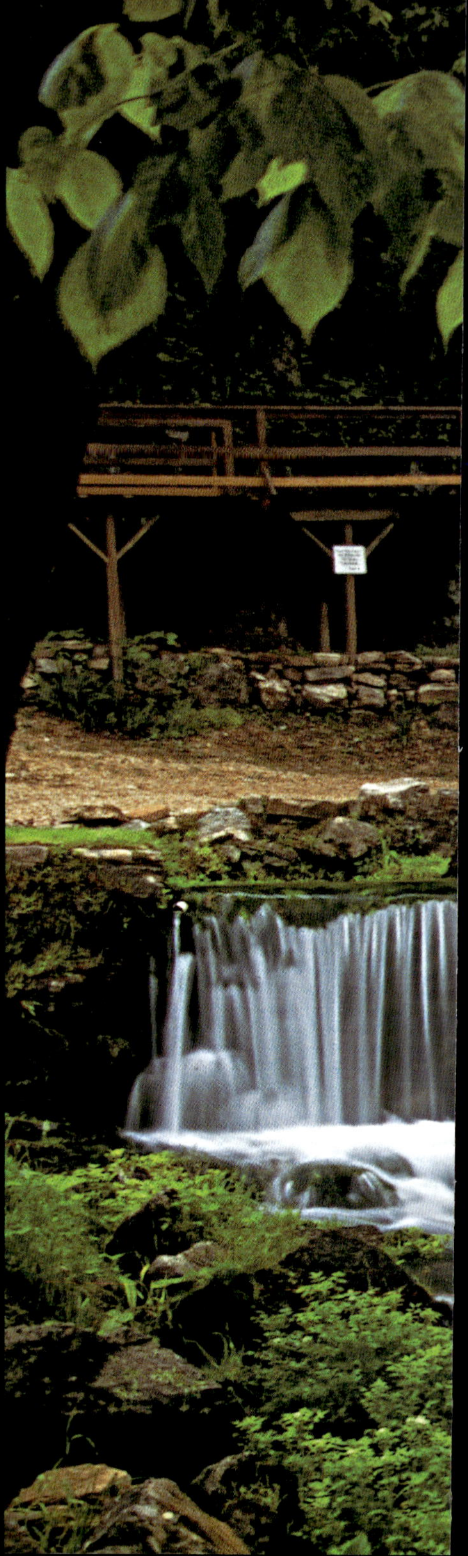

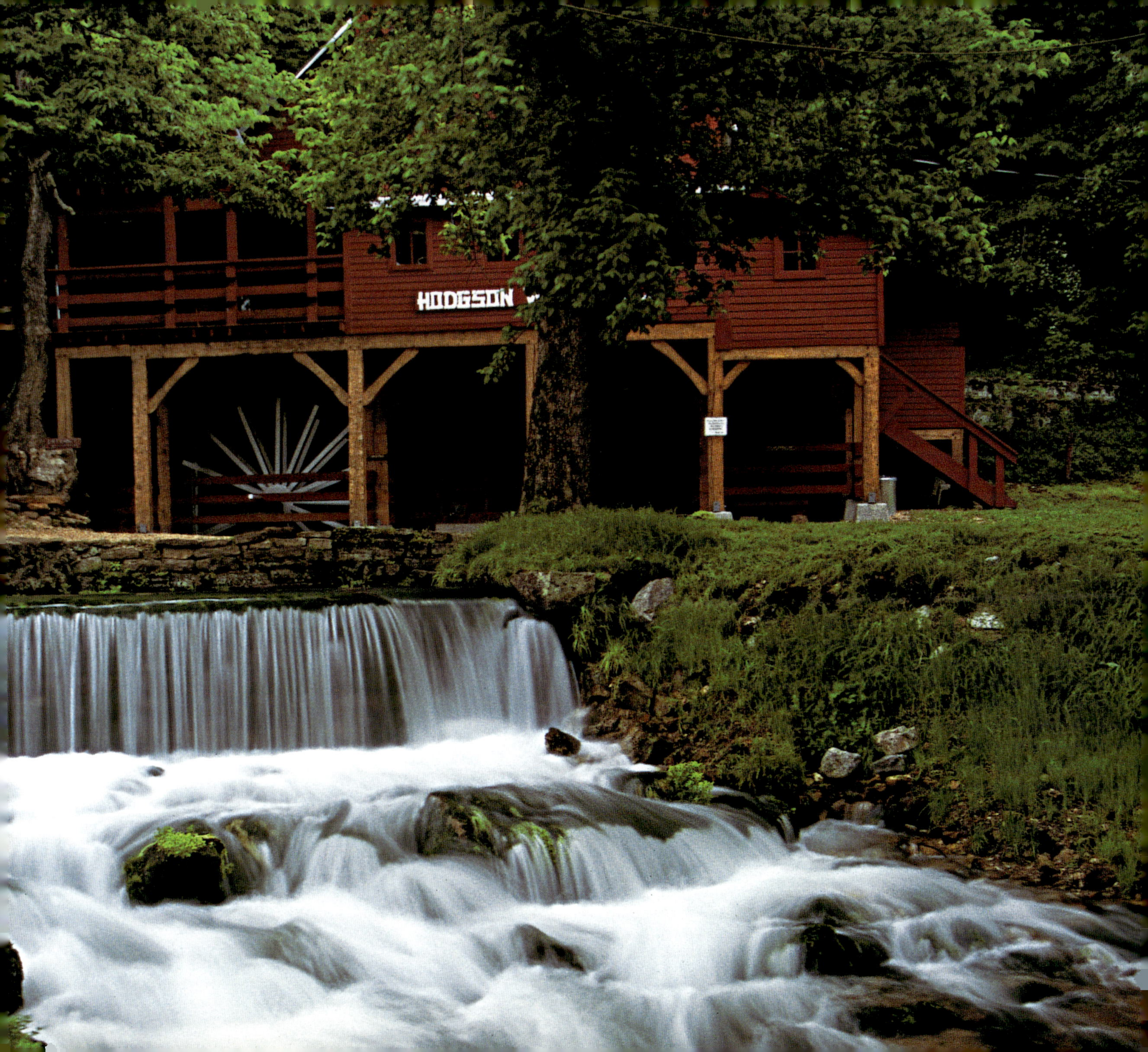
HODGSON

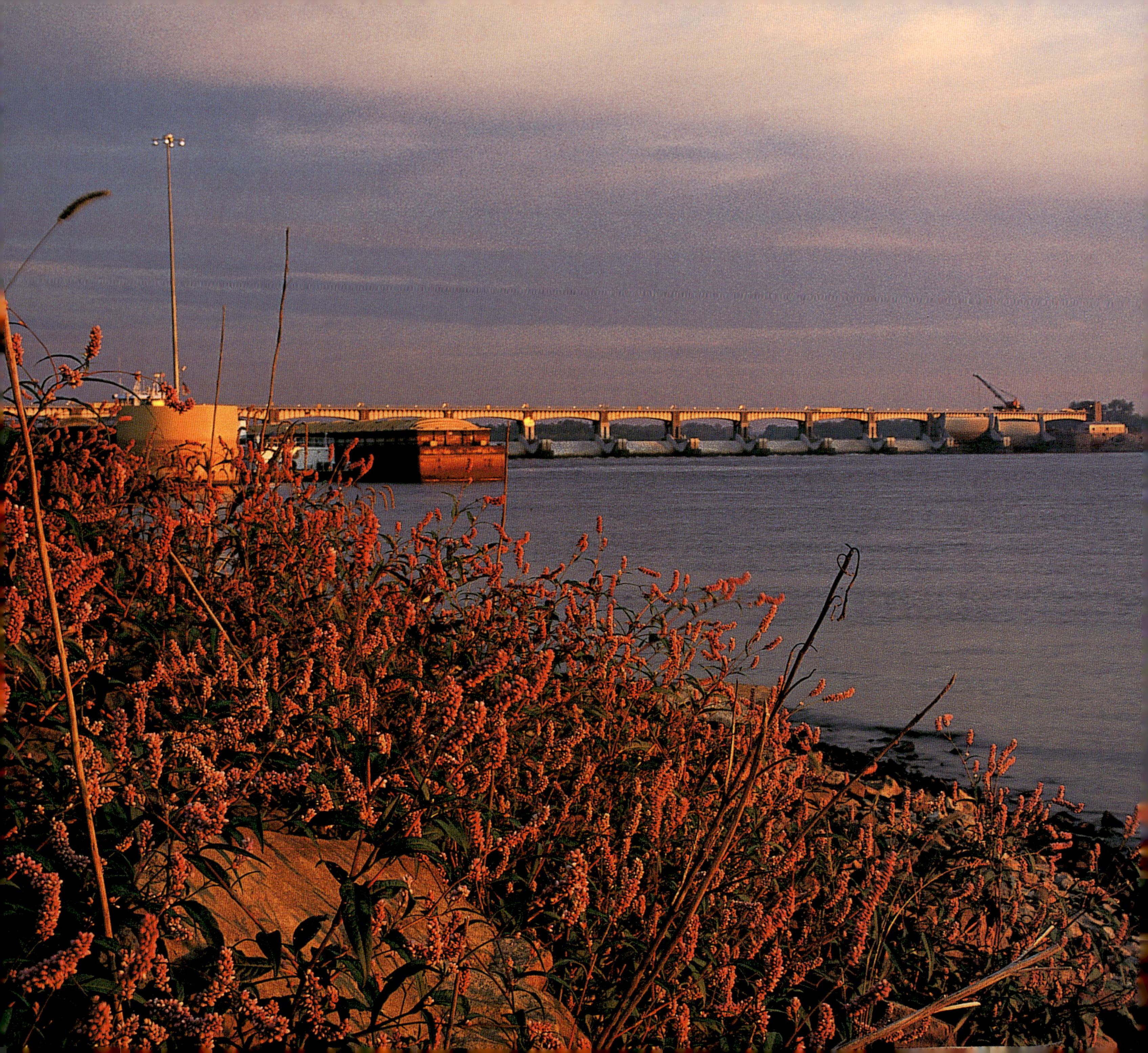

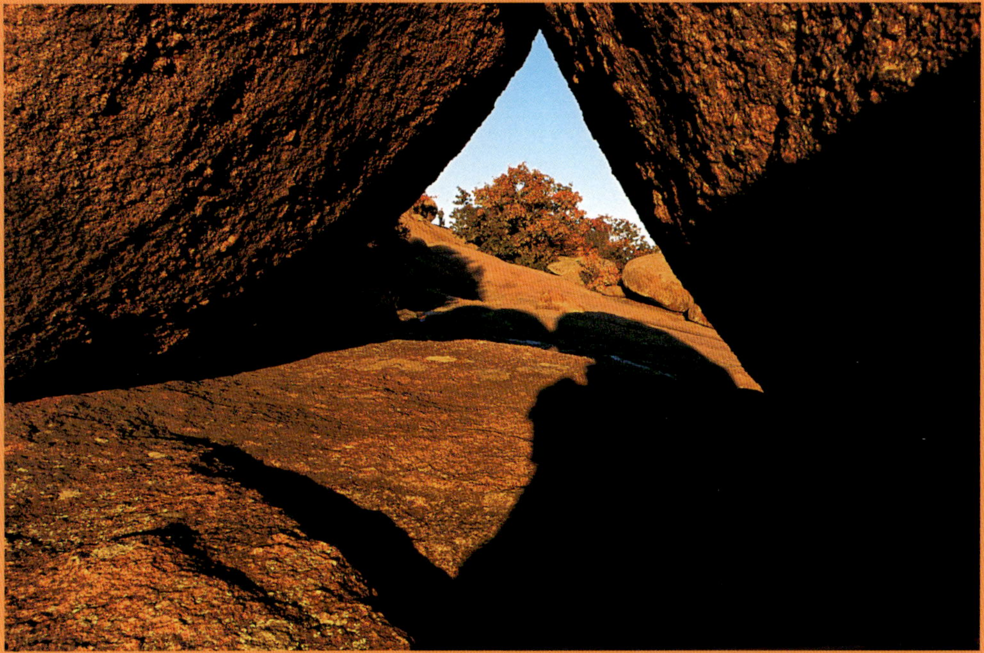

Above: Peek through gigantic boulders of granite standing end-to-end, like a line of parading elephants. The red granite is a recognizable feature of Elephant Rocks State Park, which has a mile-long footpath featuring a braille trail, as well as picnic areas.

Left: Sunrise provides a rosy hue to the area around Lock and Dam No. 24 in Clarksville. This impoundment on the Mississippi River has operated continuously since 1940. Each year, million of tons of commodities pass through the lock.

Right: The burned-out shell of Ha Ha Tonka Castle is now preserved in a 3,680-acre state park near Lake of the Ozarks. Fifteen miles of hiking trails provide views of caves, sinkholes, freshwater springs, and spectacular scenery.

Below: Winston Churchill Memorial, located at Westminster College in Fulton, honors the life and legacy of one of the twentieth century's great leaders. The museum is full of artifacts and informative exhibits.

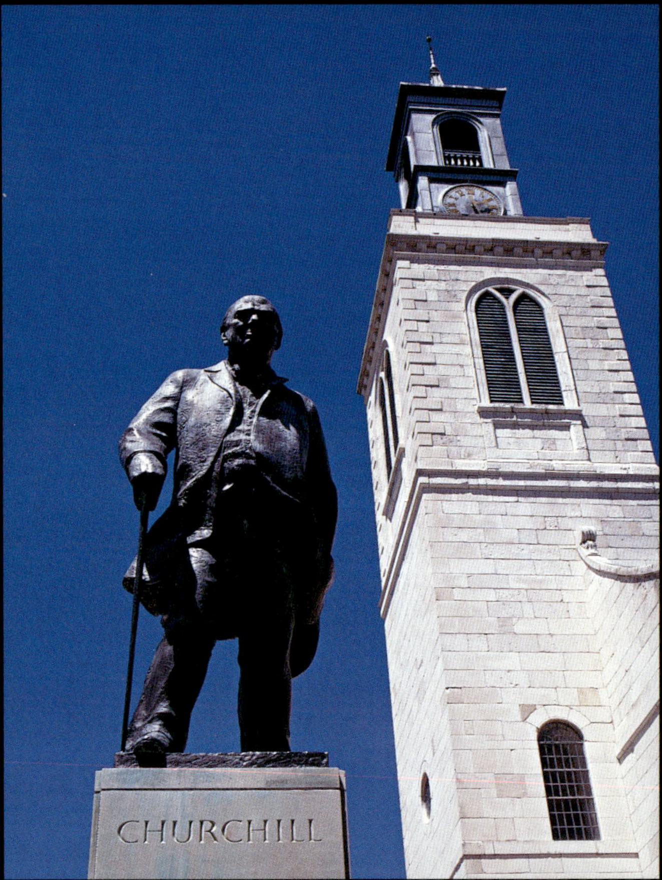

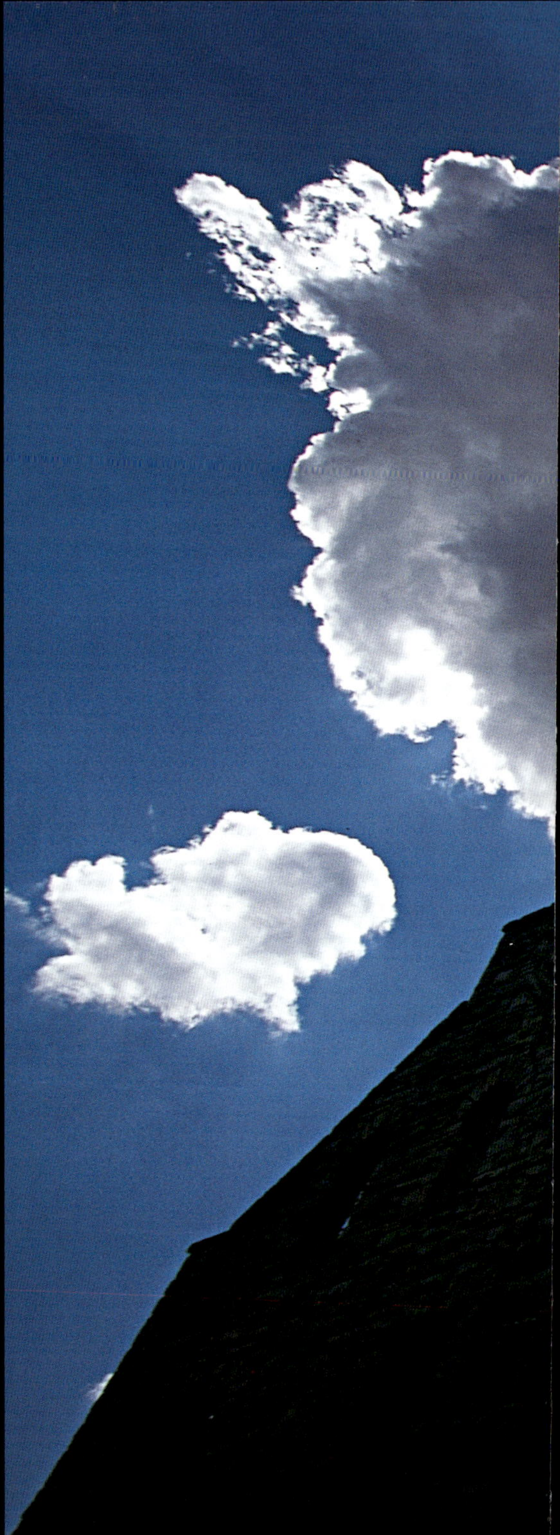

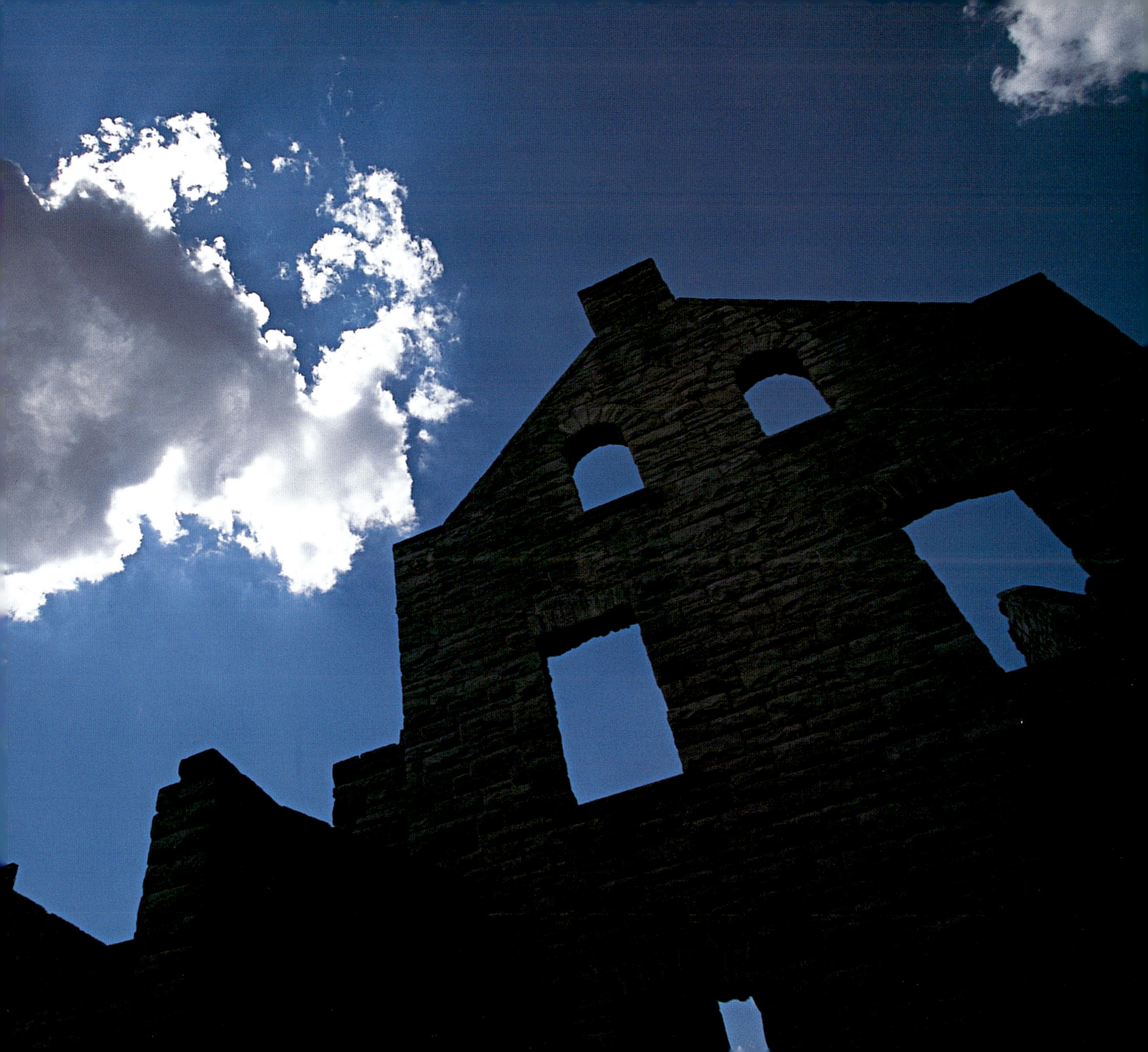

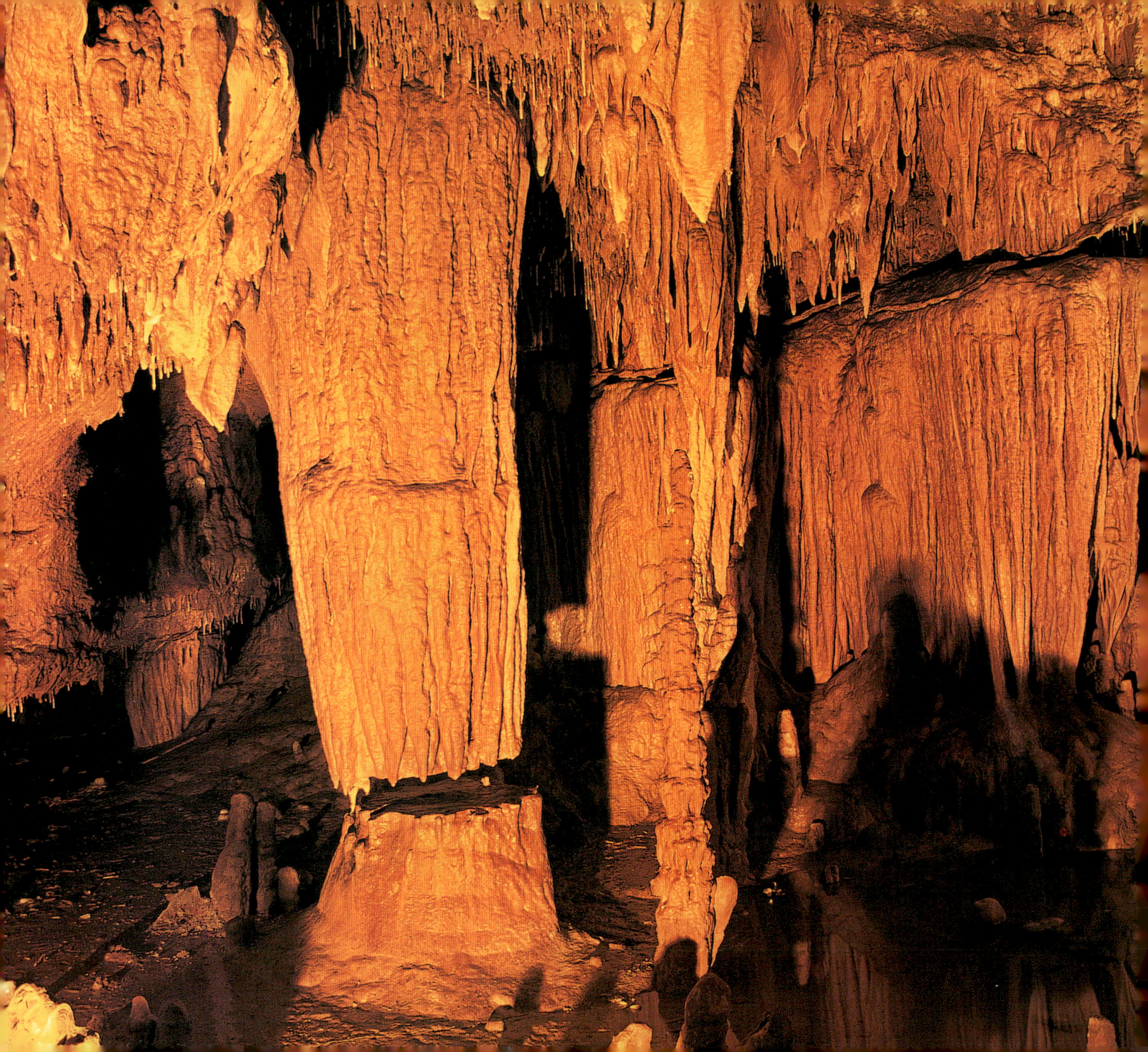

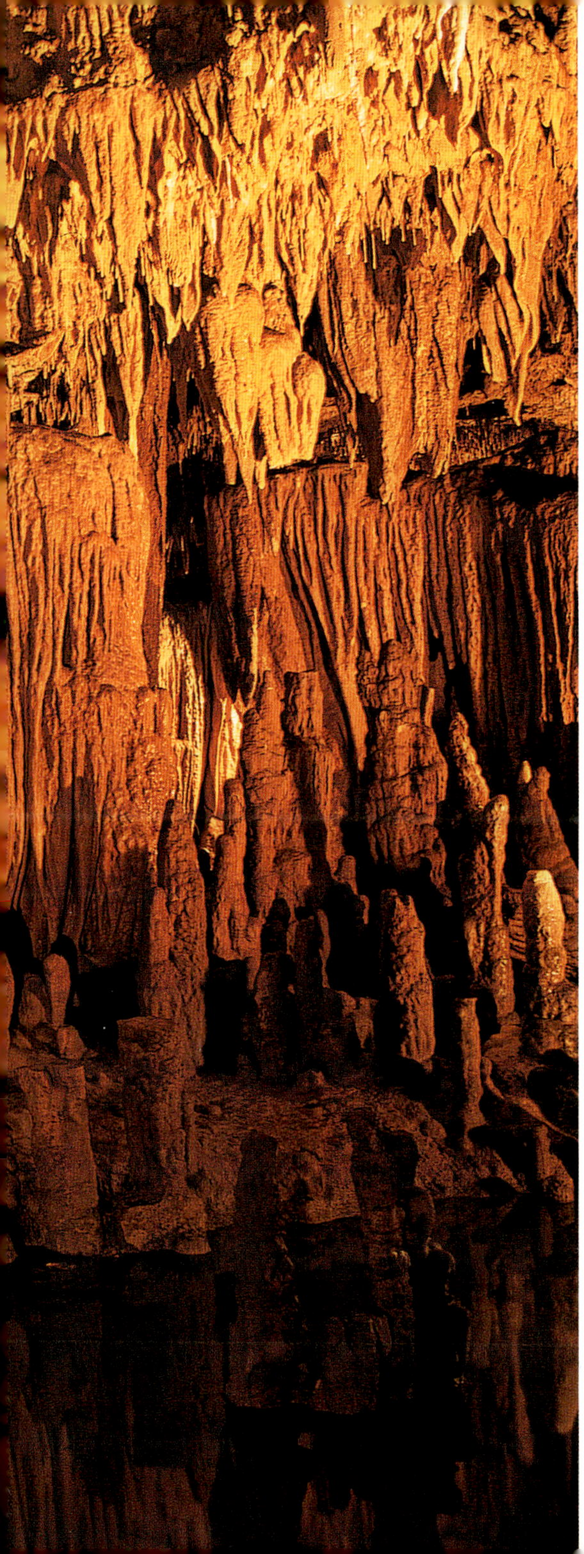

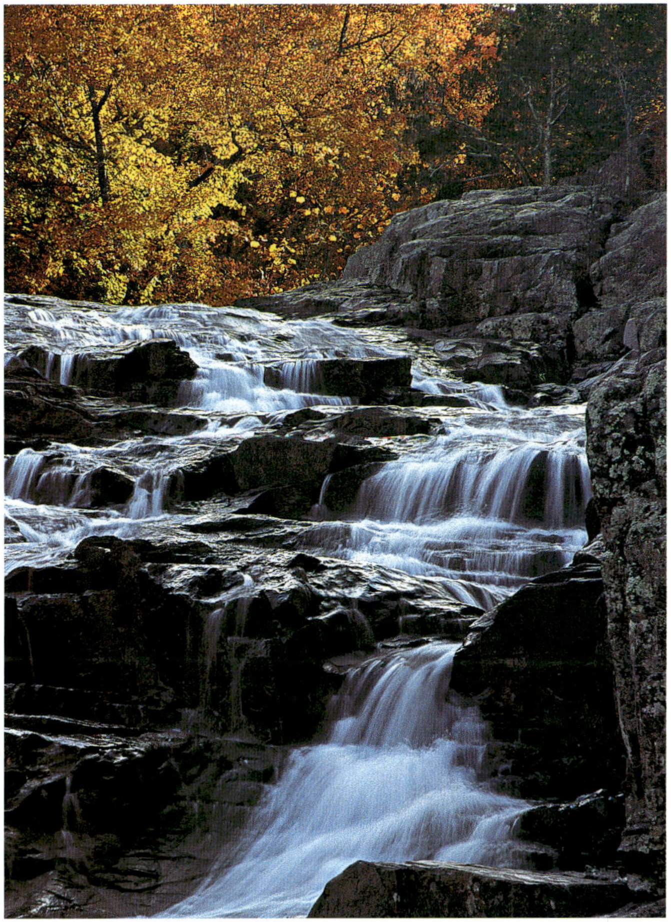

Above: Rocky Falls tumbles 40 feet down the slopes of pink and purple porphyry in Stegall Mountain Natural Area. Missouri has more than 2,000 species of native plants that occupy its diverse habitats, from wetlands to prairies to savannas.

Left: With more than 5,500 natural caves, Missouri's reputation as the Cave State is warranted. Onondaga Cave State Park displays amazing limestone formations of stalactites, stalagmites, and flowstones.

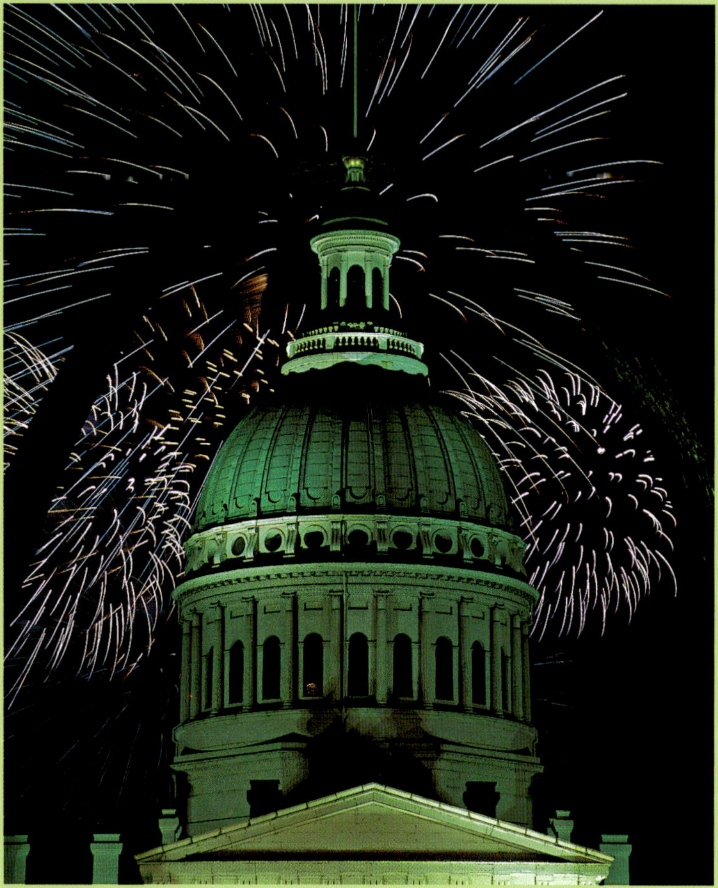

Above: St. Louis celebrates the 4th of July in a big way, The fireworks display lighting the night sky over the Old Courthouse is seen here from Kiener Plaza.

Right: The new Busch Stadium, which opened in 2006 and holds 49,676 fans, is home to the St. Louis Cardinals. The original stadium hosted six World Series, with the Cardinals winning in 1967 and 1982. The Cardinals won the 2006 World Series, a real triumph in their brand new stadium.

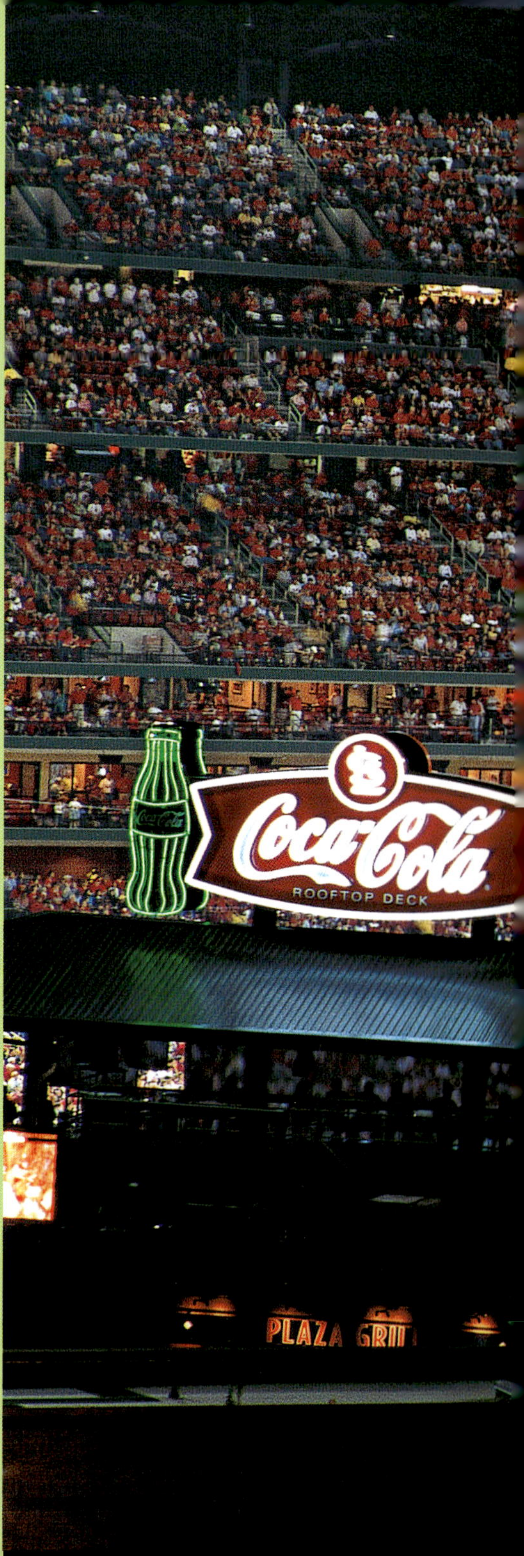

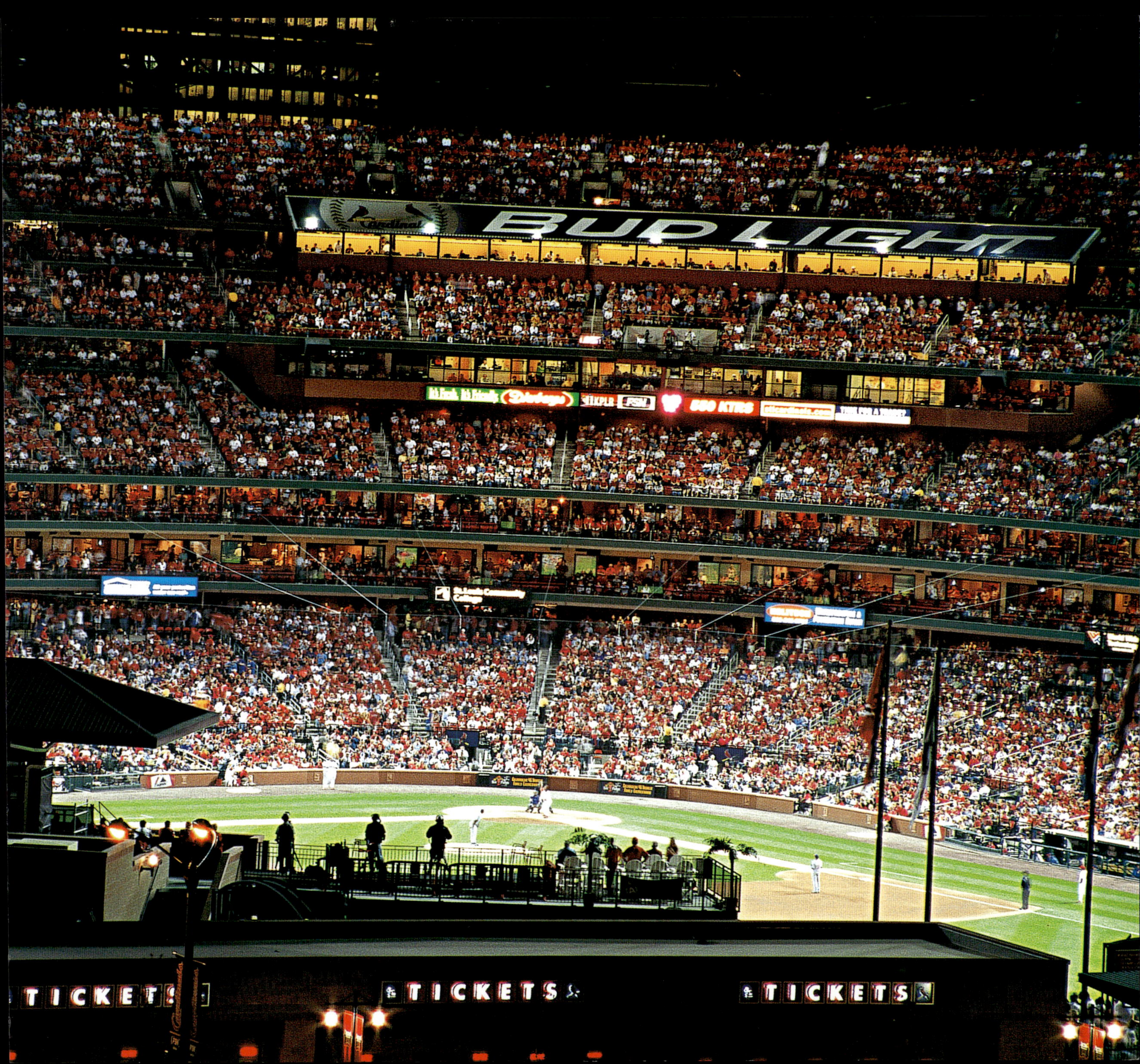
BUD LIGHT
TICKETS
TICKETS
TICKETS

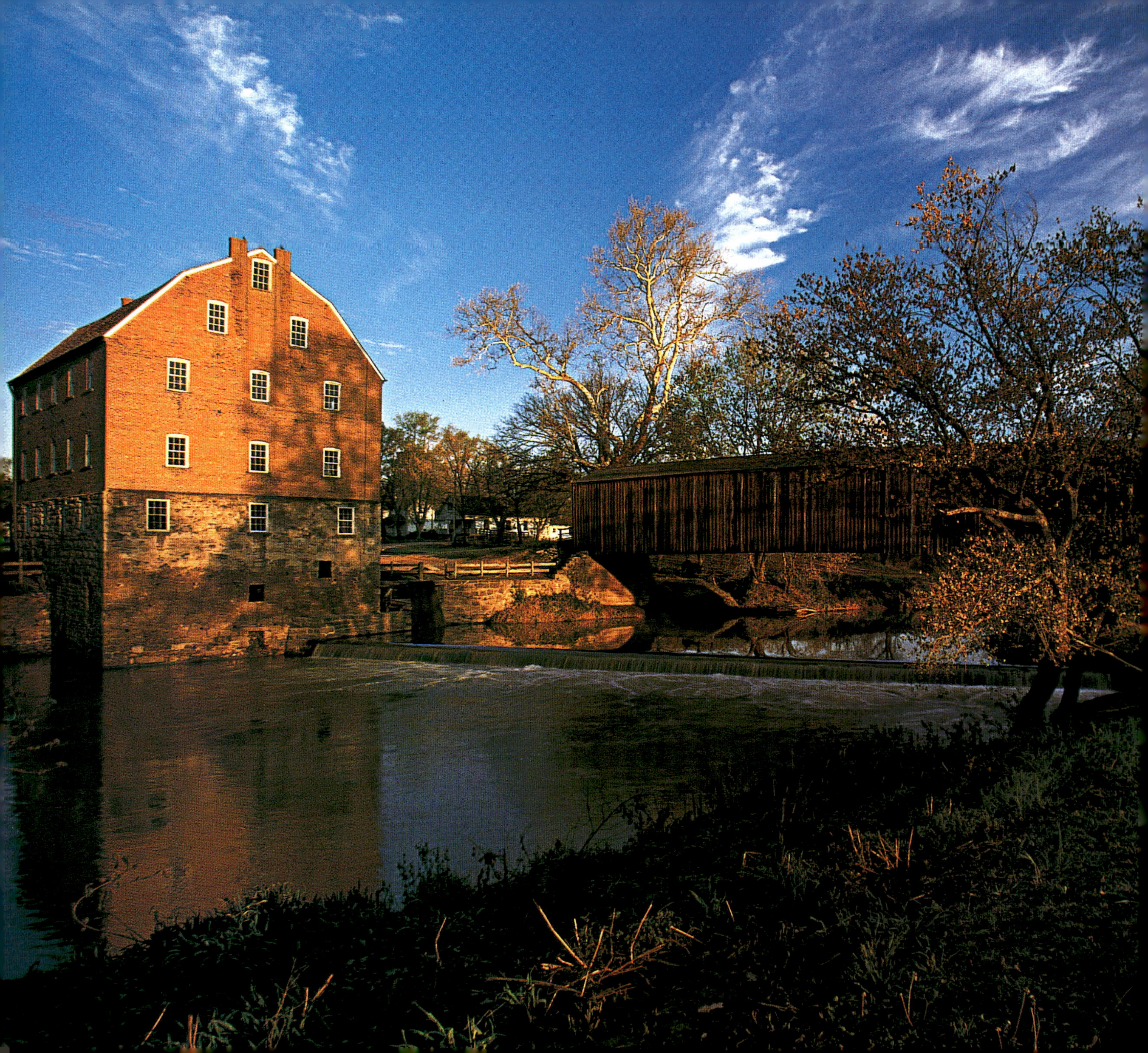

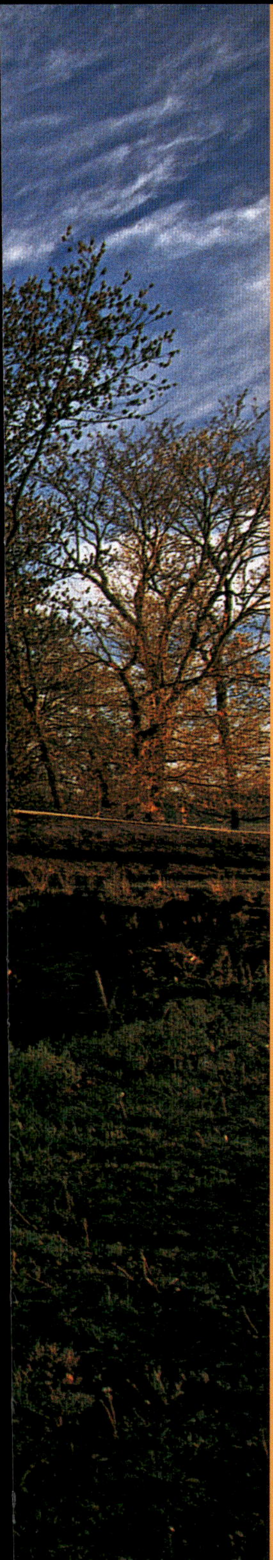

Left: The 140-foot Burfordville Covered Bridge leads across the Whitewater River to the imposing stone and brick Bollinger Mill, now a state historic site. Milling began in 1858, and visitors to Cape Girardeau can still watch corn being ground into meal here.

Below: Grapevines seen from Hermann Hill Vineyard & Inn rest after the harvest, bathed in the glow of a low winter sun.

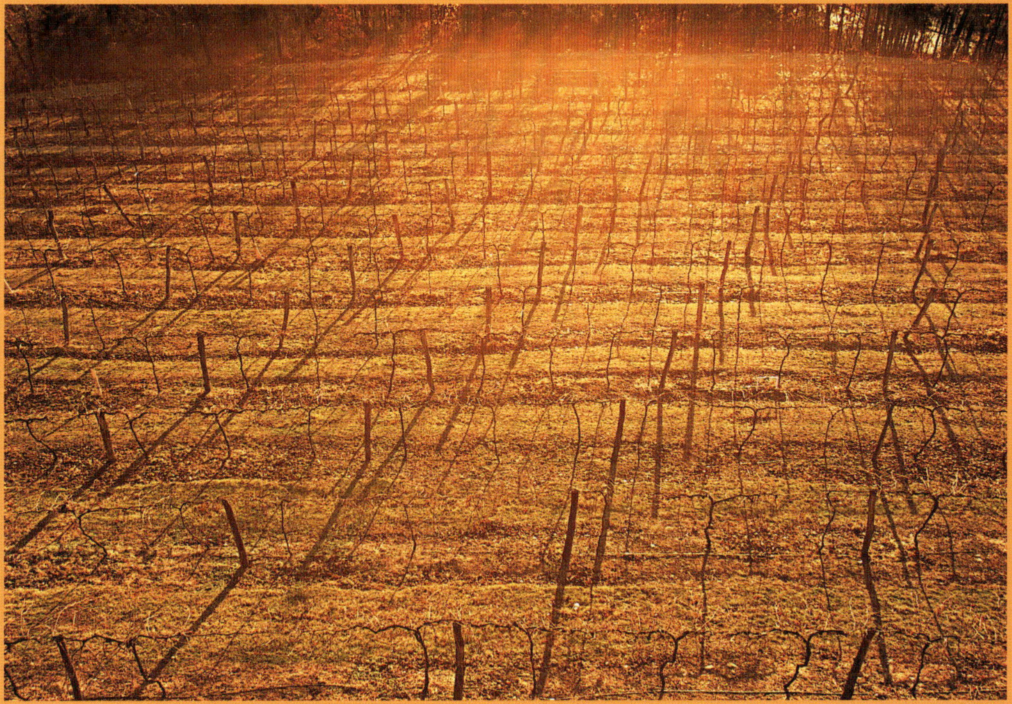

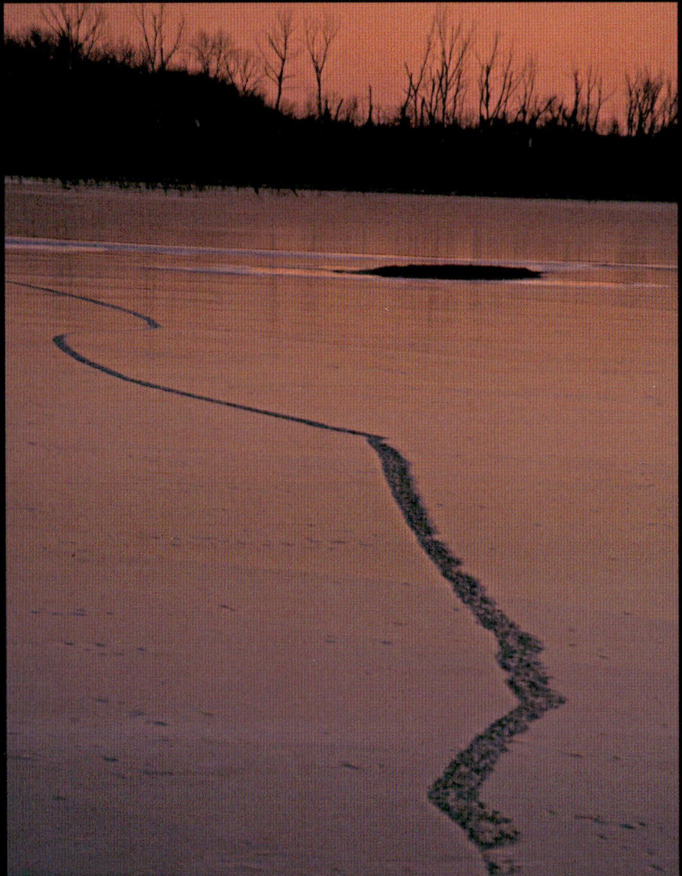

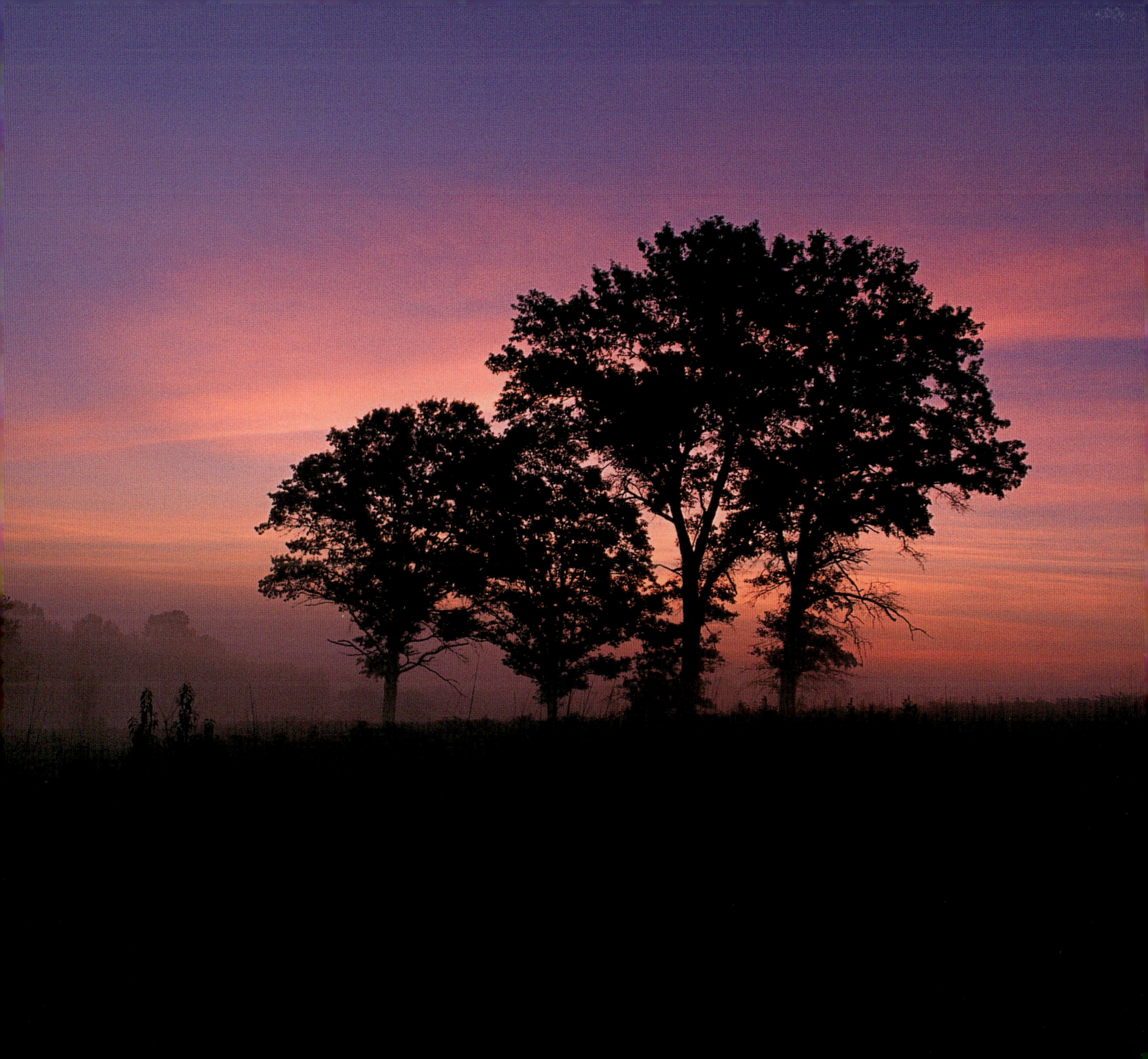

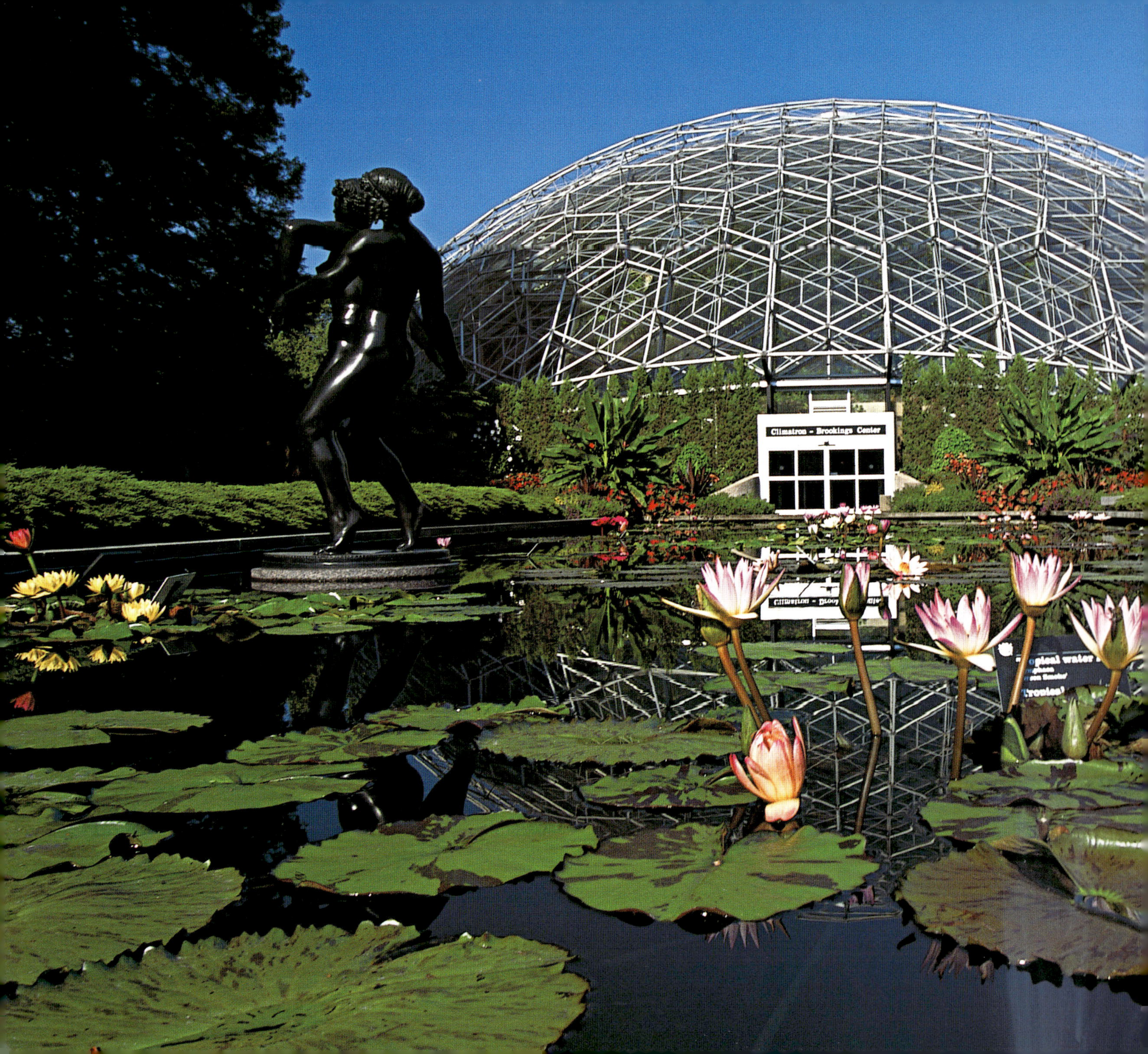
Climatron - Brookings Center

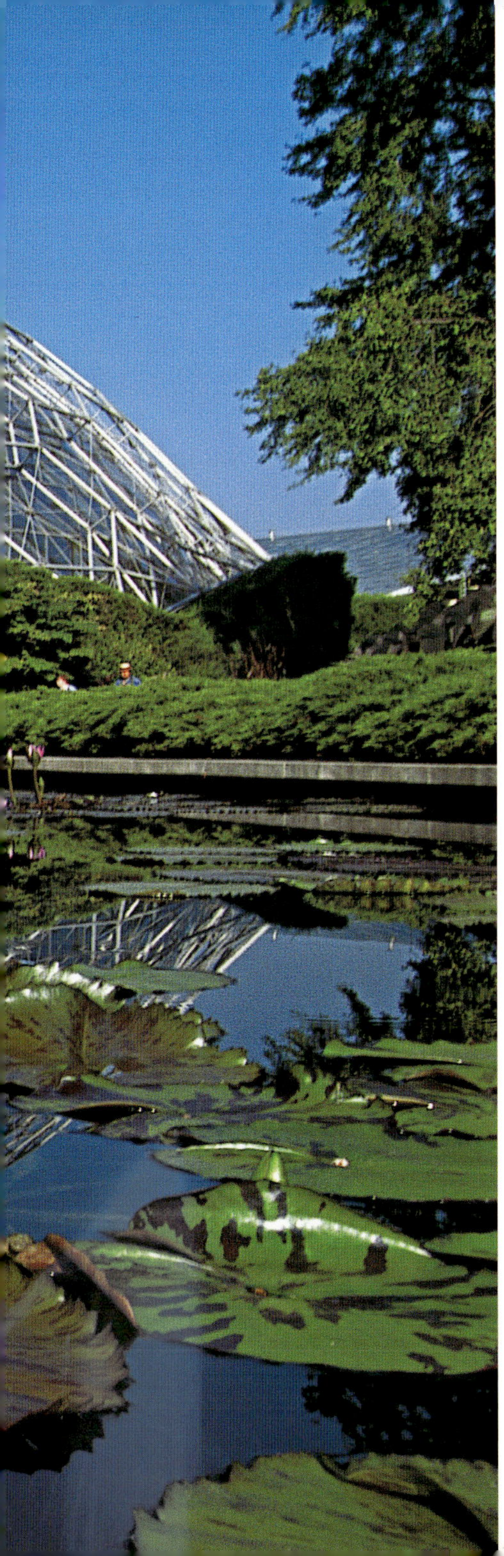

Left: Water lilies reach for the sun in the pond outside the Climatron in the Missouri Botanical Garden. This is one of the first geodesic dome conservatories ever built in the nation; in 1976 the dome was designated one of the 100 most-significant architectural achievements in U.S. history.

Below: Narcissus bloom on the slope below the Arrow Rock Lyceum Theatre, located in a former Baptist church built in 1872. This national historic landmark showcases Missouri's oldest professional regional live theatre.

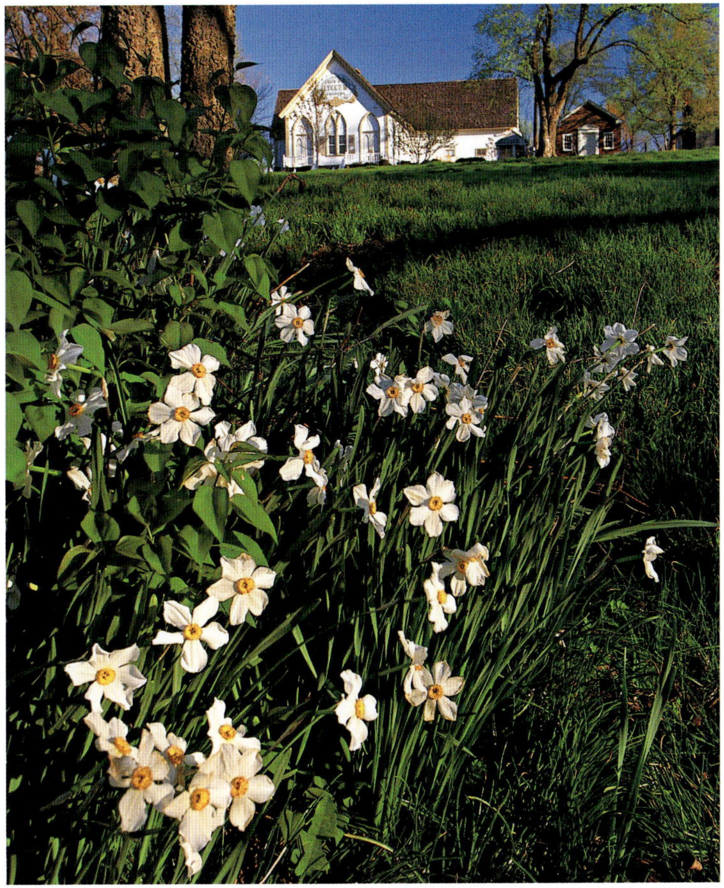

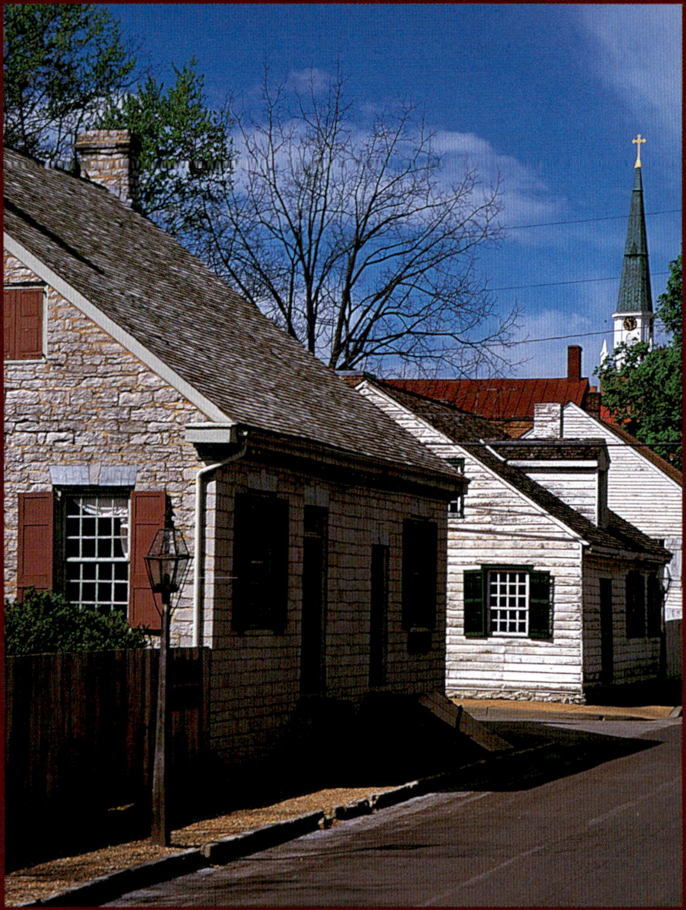

Above: Felix Valle House was built in 1818, in Ste. Genevieve. This American-Federal–style home/mercantile has been restored and furnished to reflect life in the 1830s.

Right: Every summer, Watkins Woolen Mill State Park in Lawson offers its Living History Farm Program, re-creating a family at work and play in the 1870s.

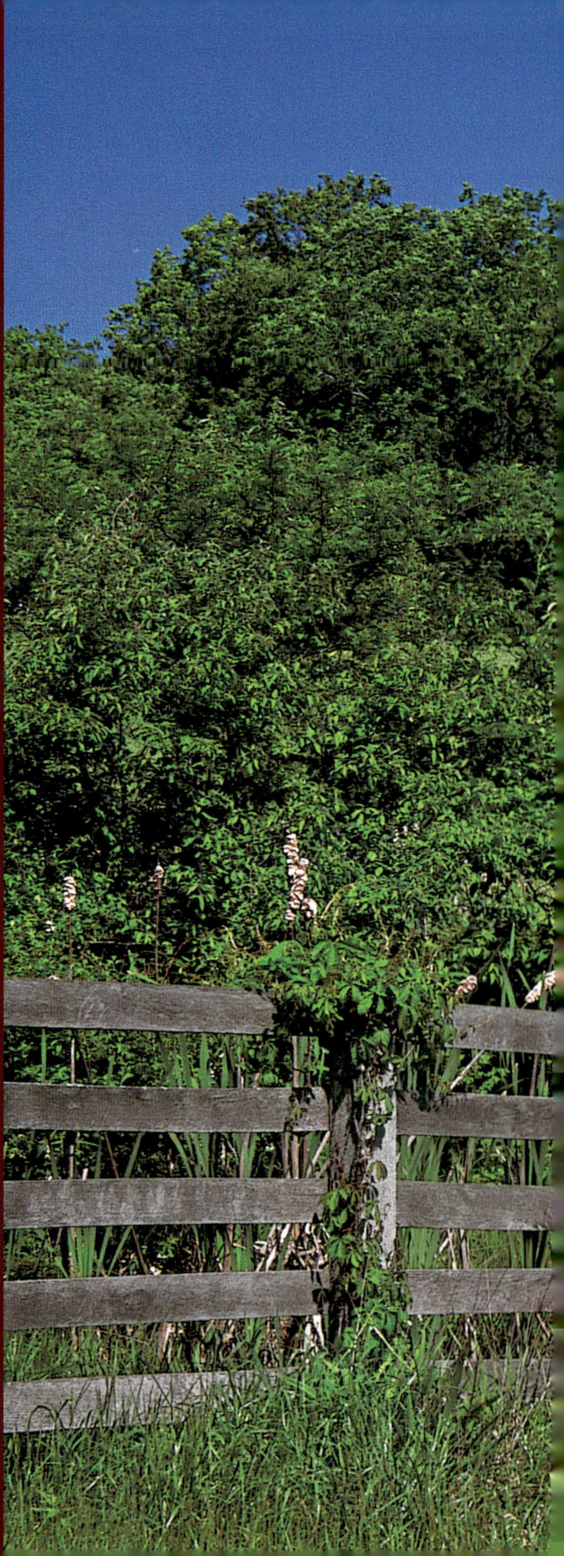

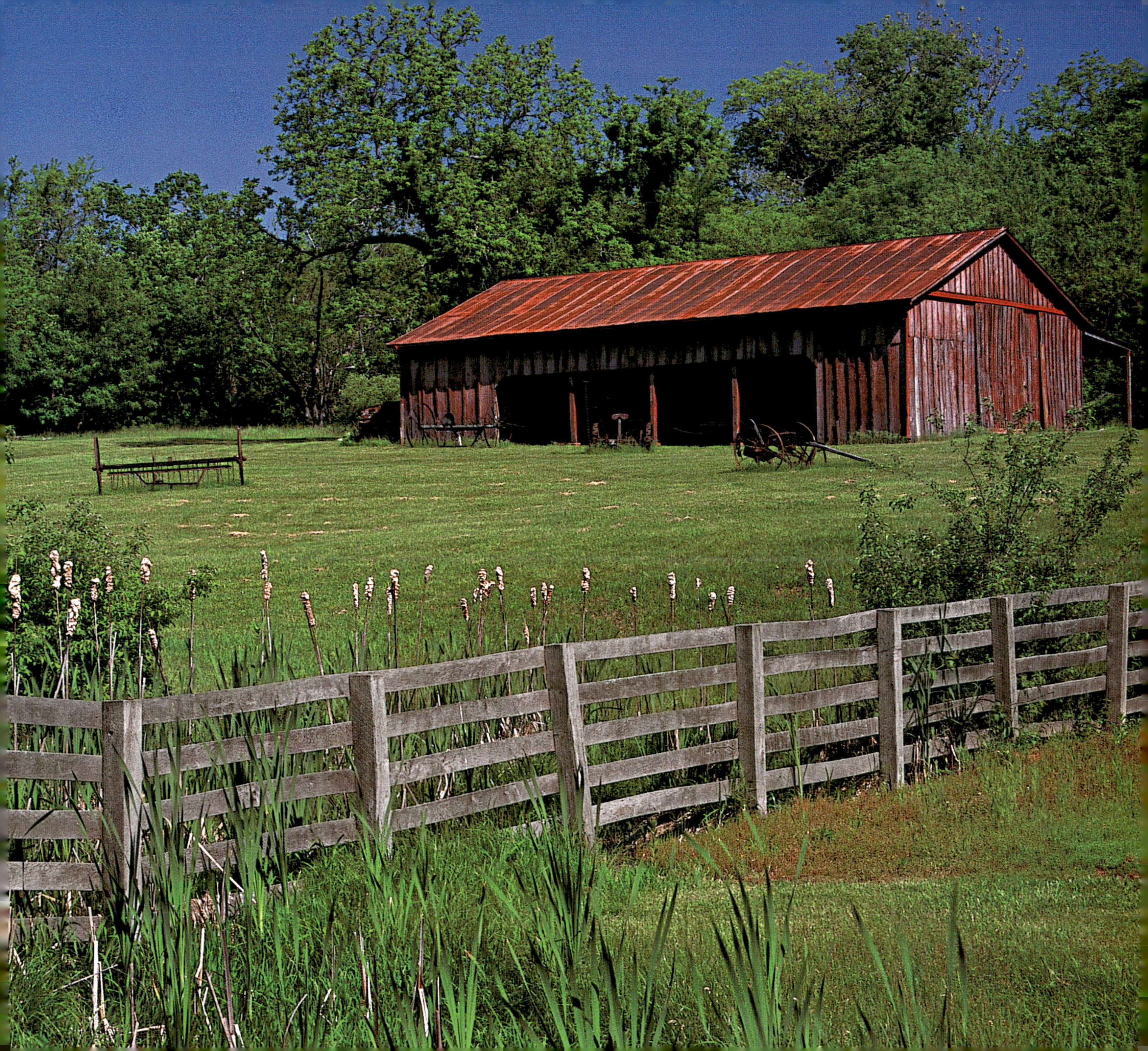

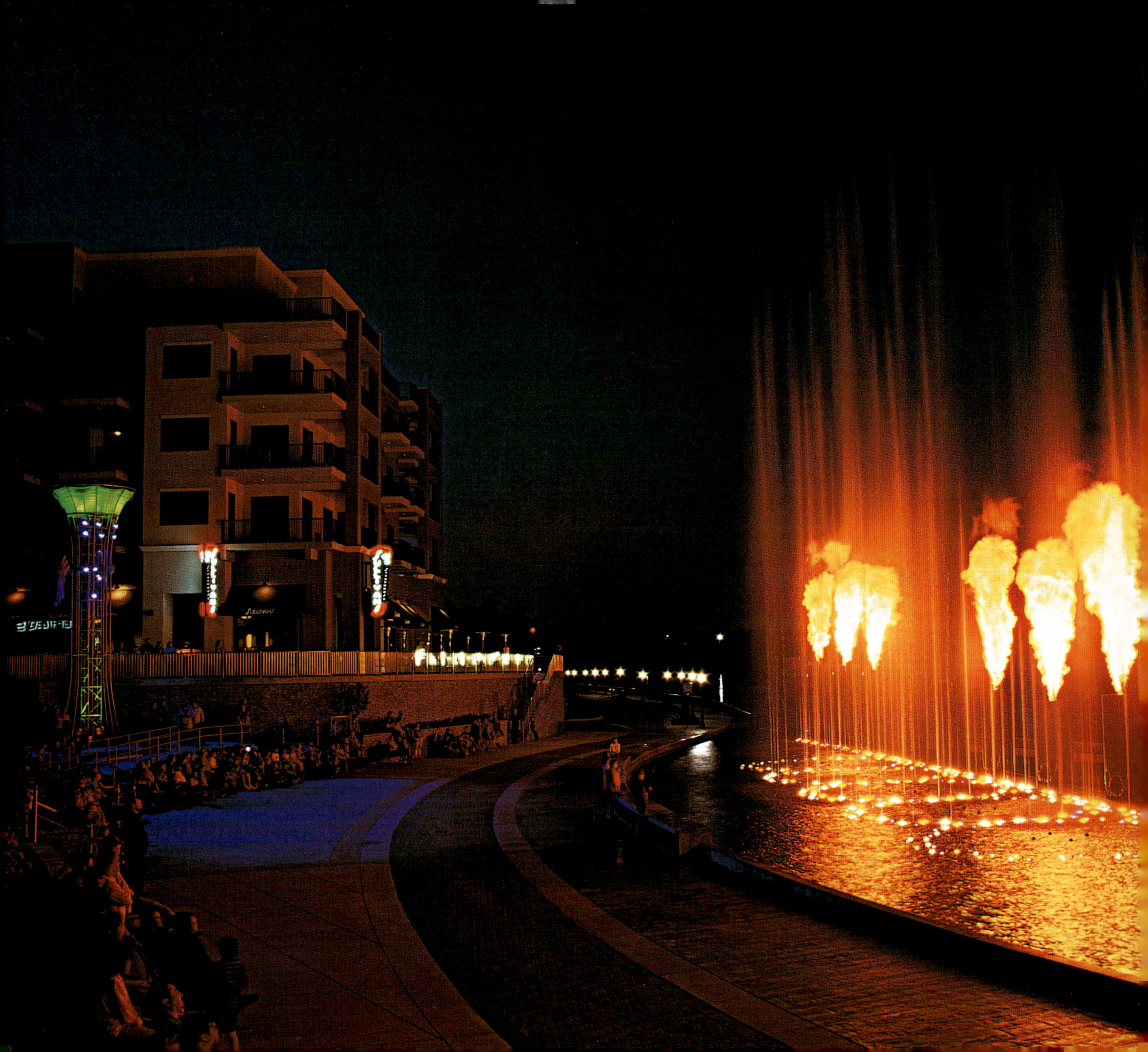

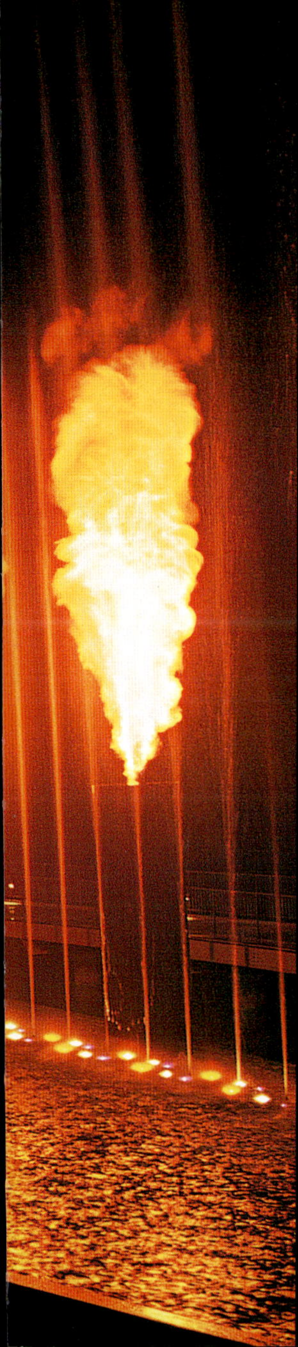

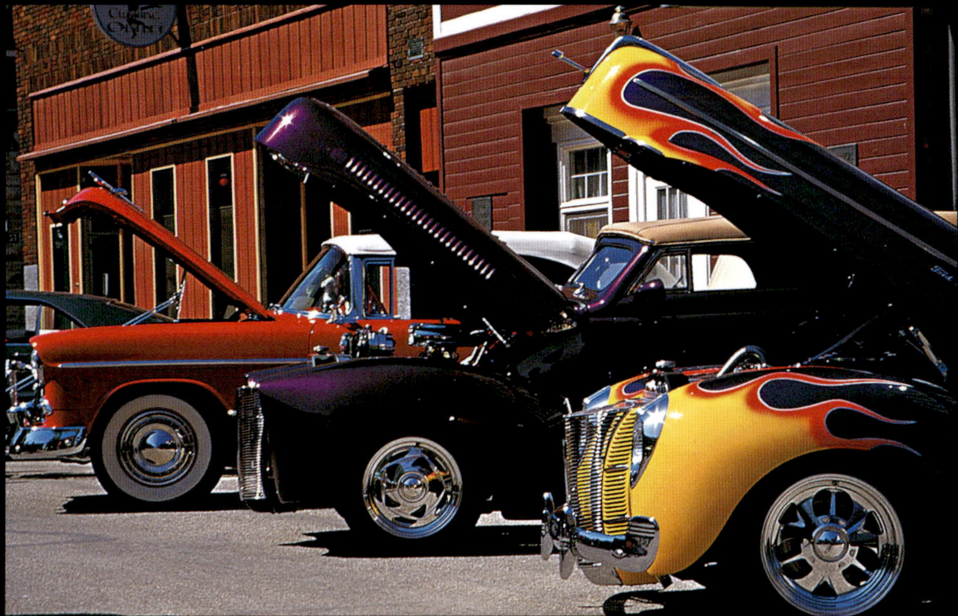

Above: Proud owners lift the hoods to show off their meticulously restored antique cars and roadsters in Sedalia.

Left: Branson Landing provides a show of lights, fire, and water that dazzles onlookers. The Town Square has live performances that range from young talent to Motown singers to professional symphonies.

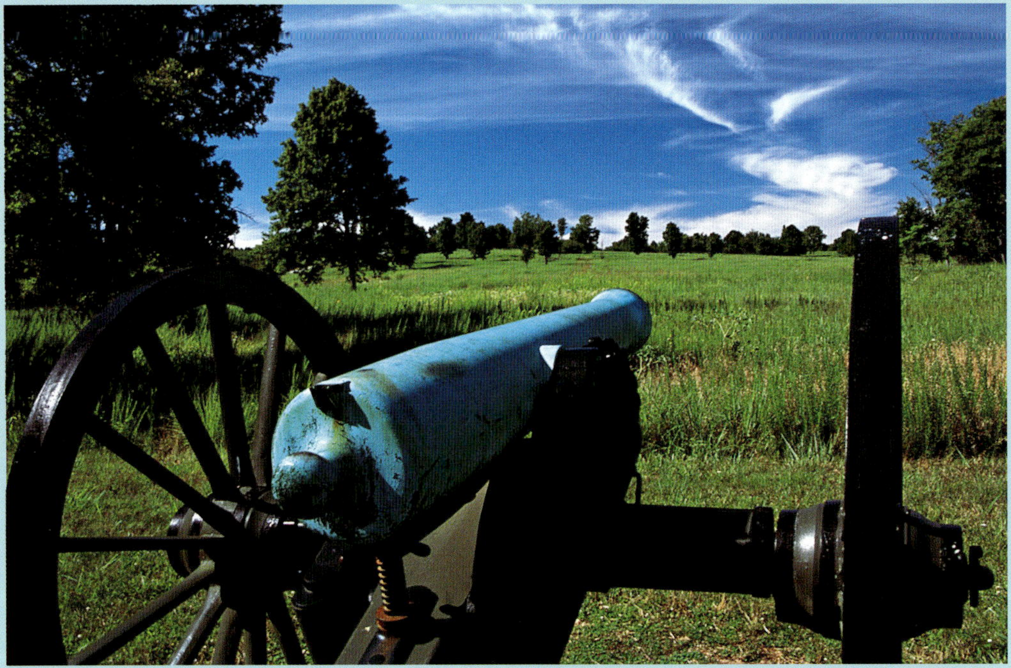

Above: Wilson's Creek National Battlefield in Springfield commemorates the site of the Civil War's first major battle fought west of the Mississippi River.

Right: The Mississippi River demarcates the state line between Missouri and Illinois. Here, a bridge on Highway 54 leaves eastern Missouri's Pike County and crosses the mighty river to Illinois.

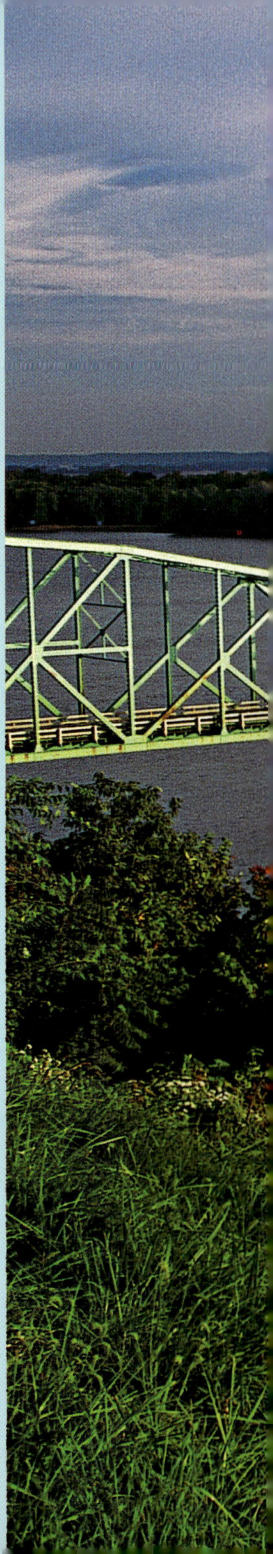

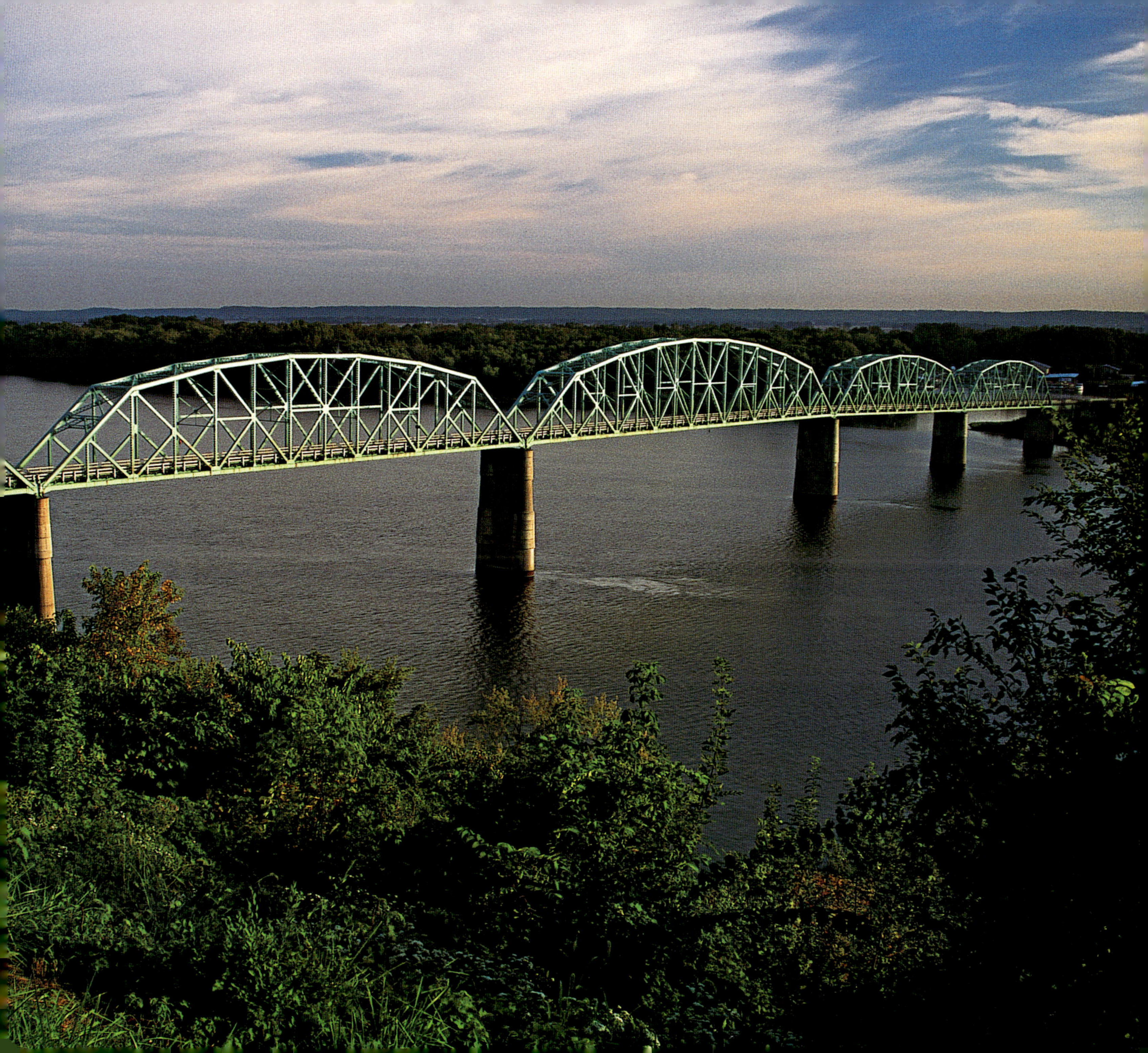

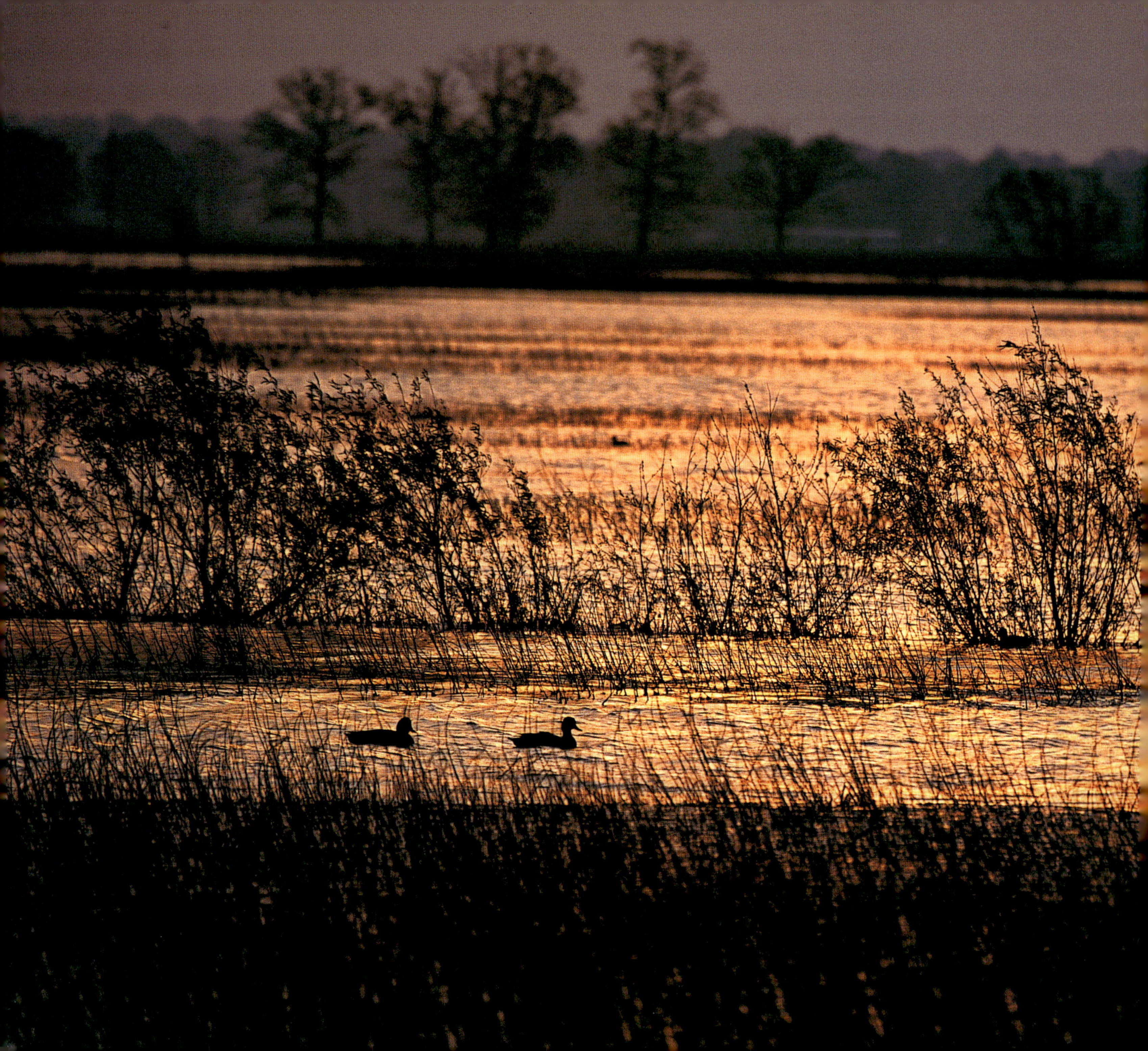

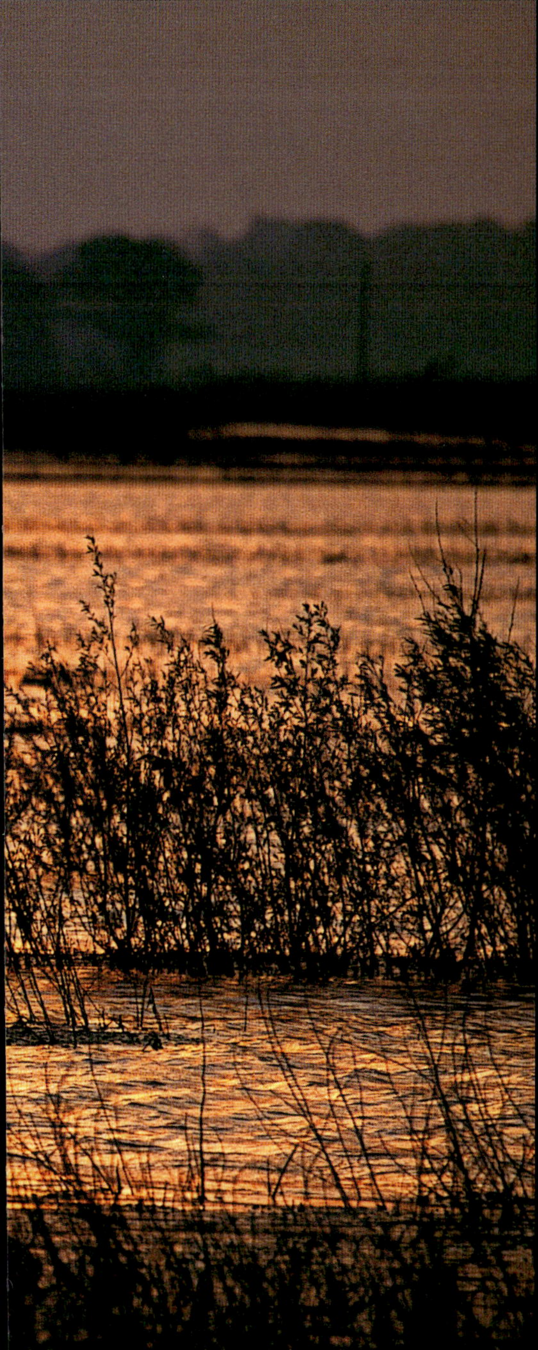

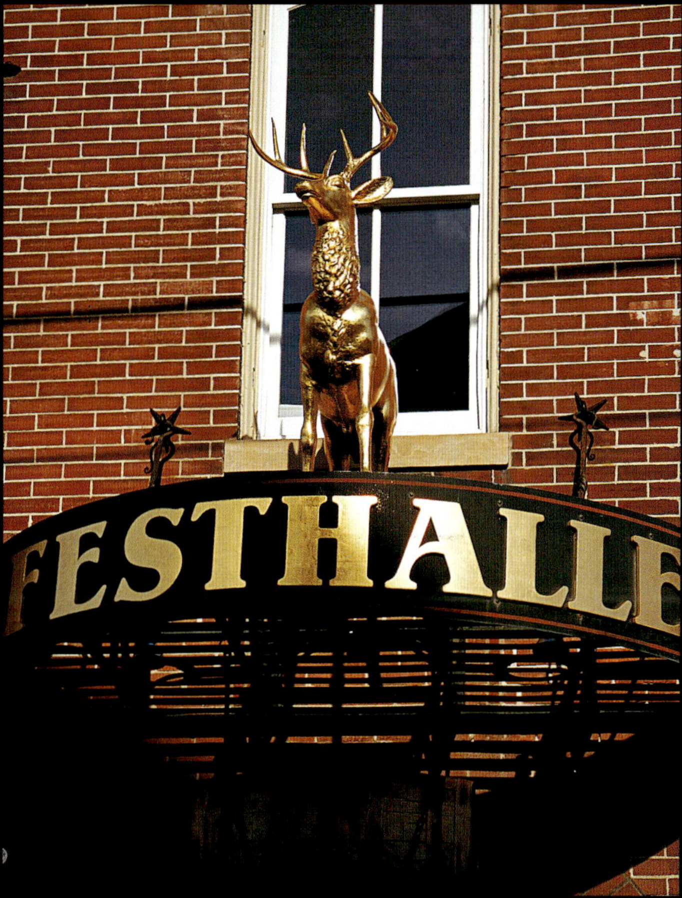

Above: The German word "fest" means a party or celebration, and this Festhalle in Hermann has indeed been a happy gathering place for the community since the 1800s.

Left: Ducks swim in the placid water of Otter Slough State Wildlife Management Area in Stoddard County.

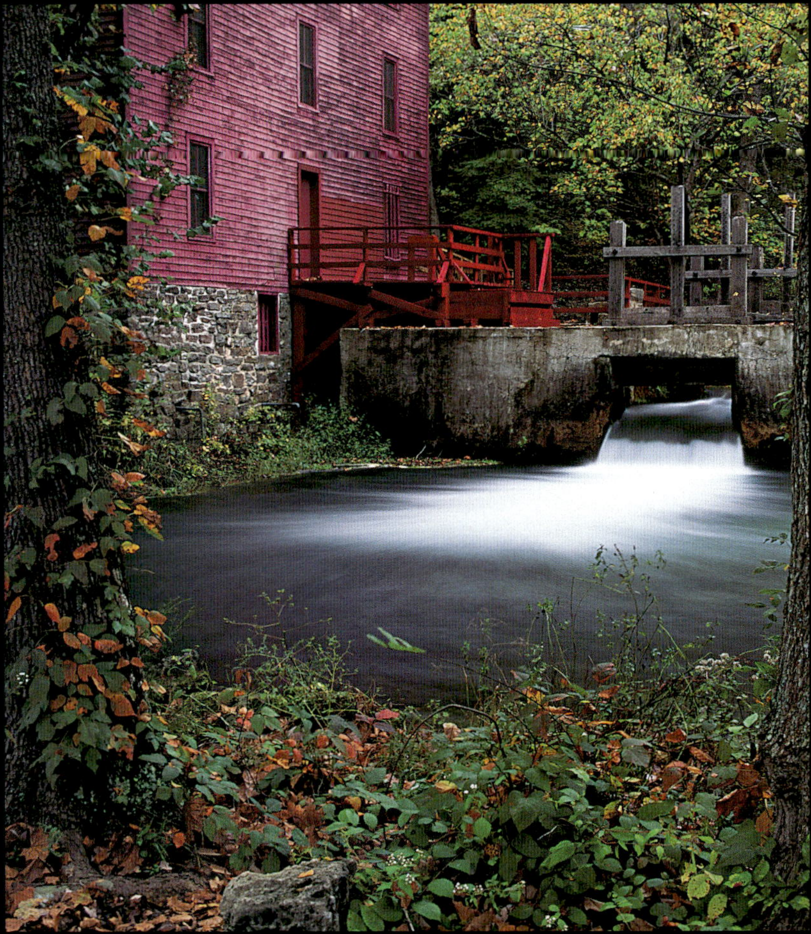

Above: Free water power turns the wheel at Alley Spring Mill, in Shannon County.

Right: Trout fishing is splendid in front of Rockbridge Mill at the Rainbow Trout Ranch. Rockbridge was settled in 1841, near the confluence of Spring Creek and Bryant Creek.

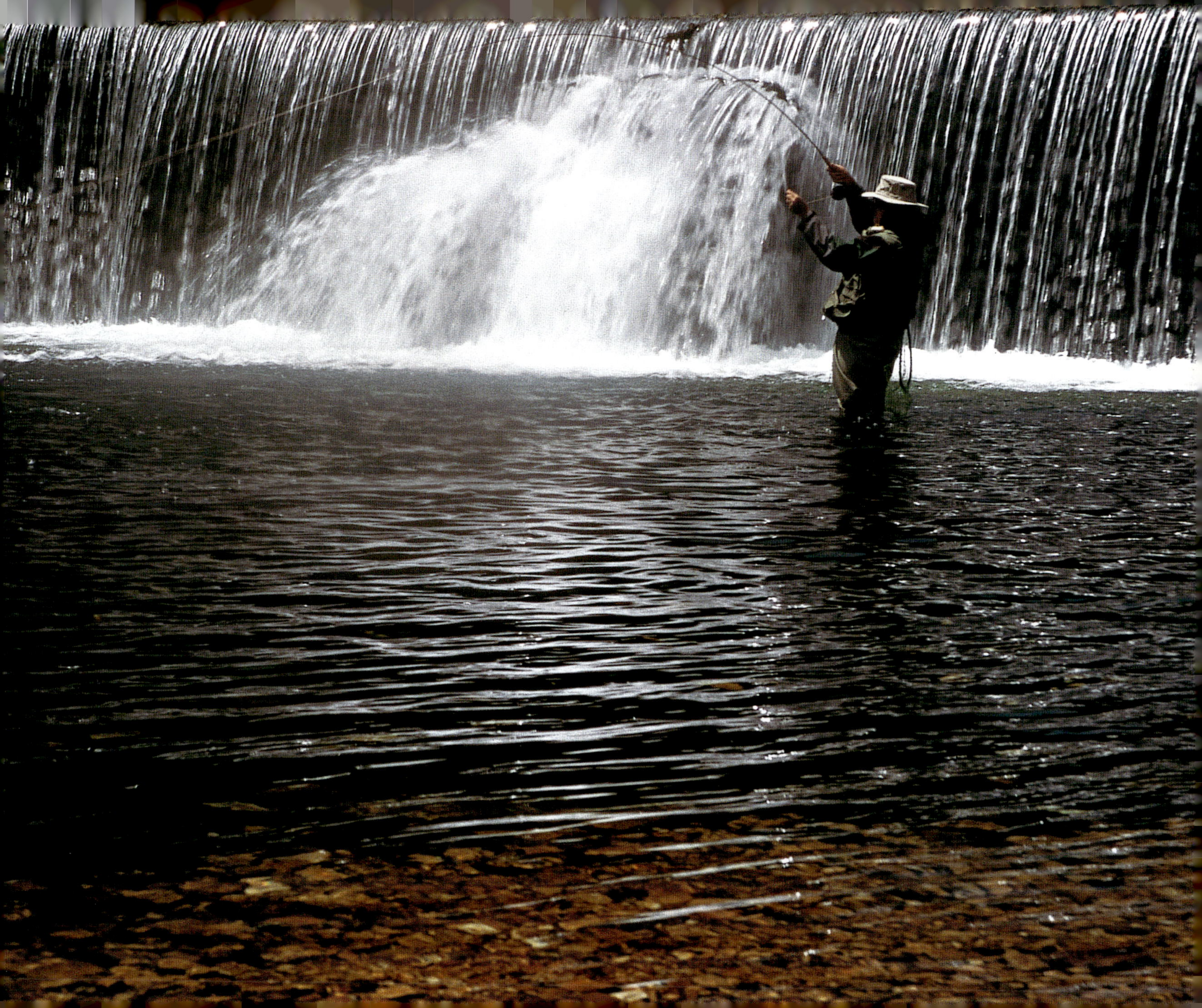

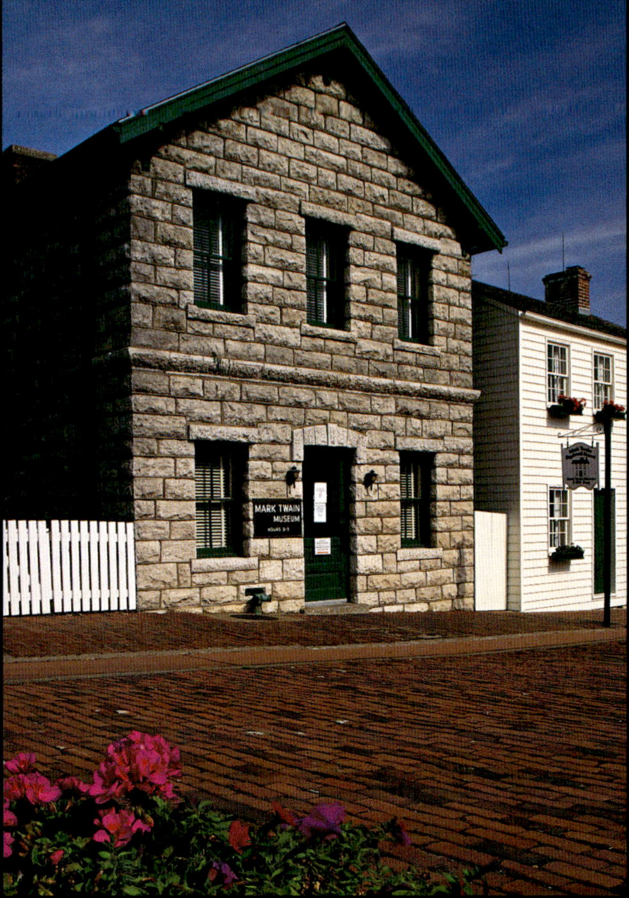

Hannibal's most famous resident was legendary author Mark Twain (1835–1910), born Samuel Clemens. His boyhood home is now part of a complex of historic houses and museums.

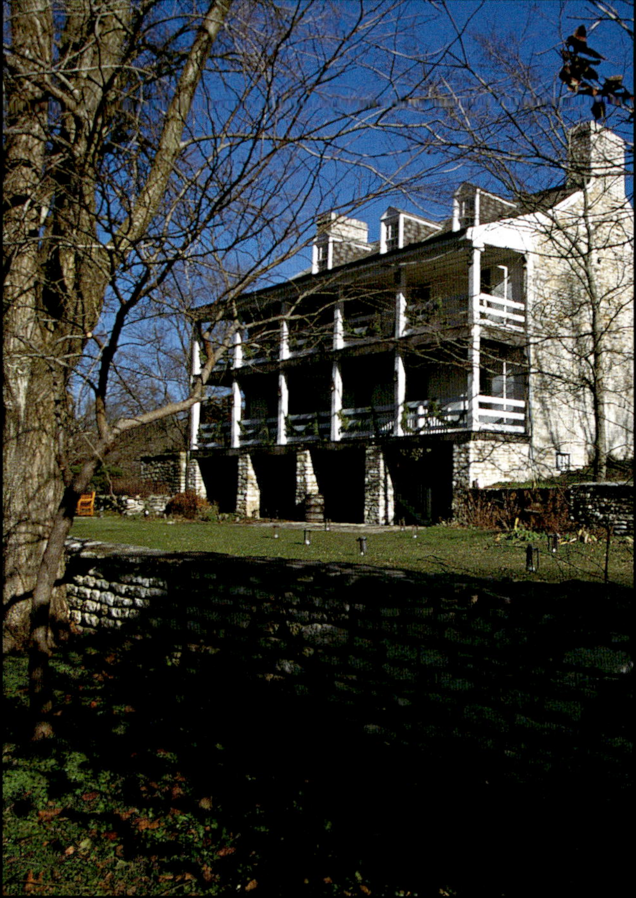

Expansive back verandas characterize the impressive limestone Daniel Boone Home in Defiance. Boone, a famous explorer and statesman, lived from 1734 to 1820.

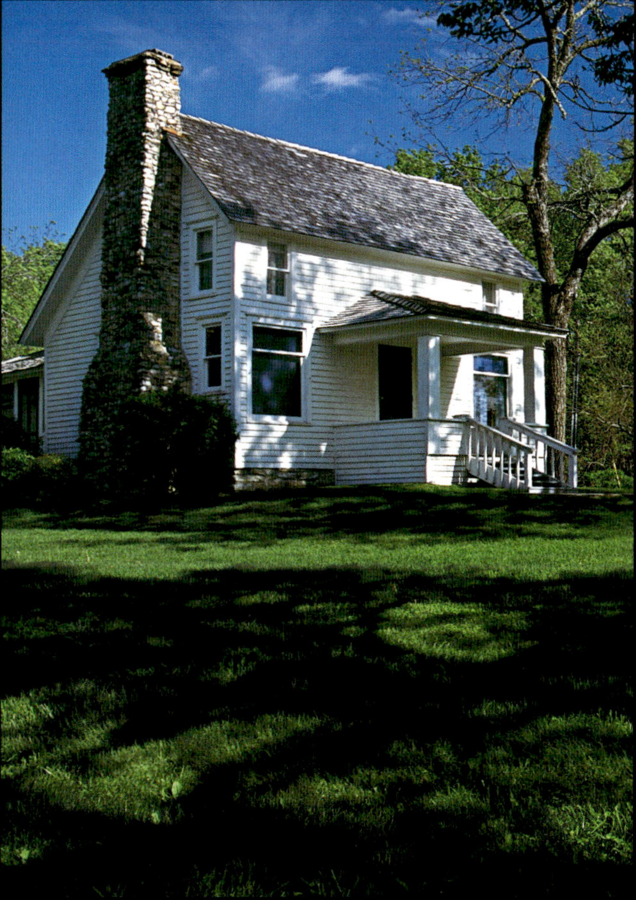

Laura Ingalls Wilder (1867–1957) lived in this home in Mansfield. Now a museum, it preserves the place where she wrote all nine of her classics centered around the book *Little House on the Prairie*.

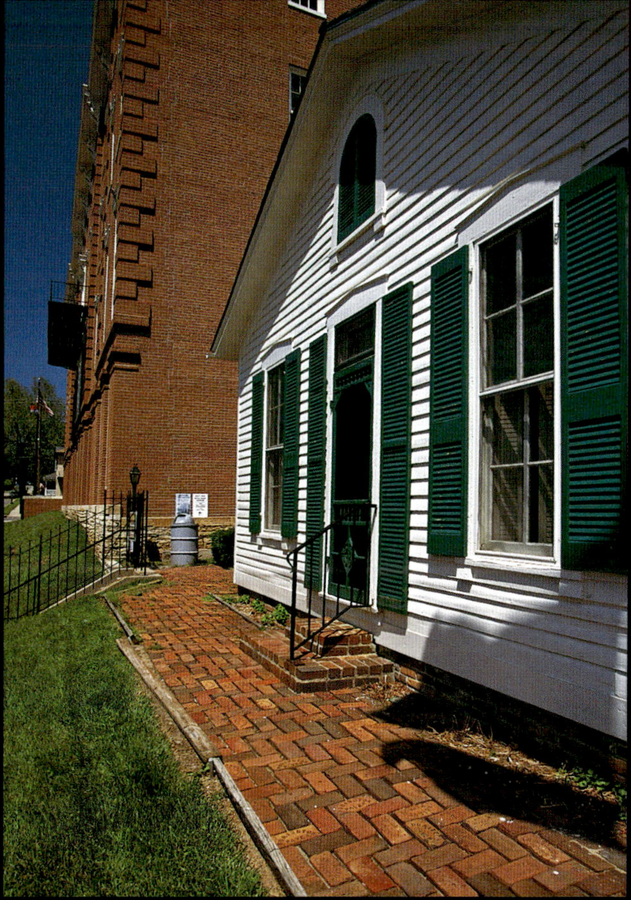

Jesse James lived his final years in this home in St. Joseph. James was a renegade and thief, legendary for his cold-blooded violence. He lived from 1847 to 1882.

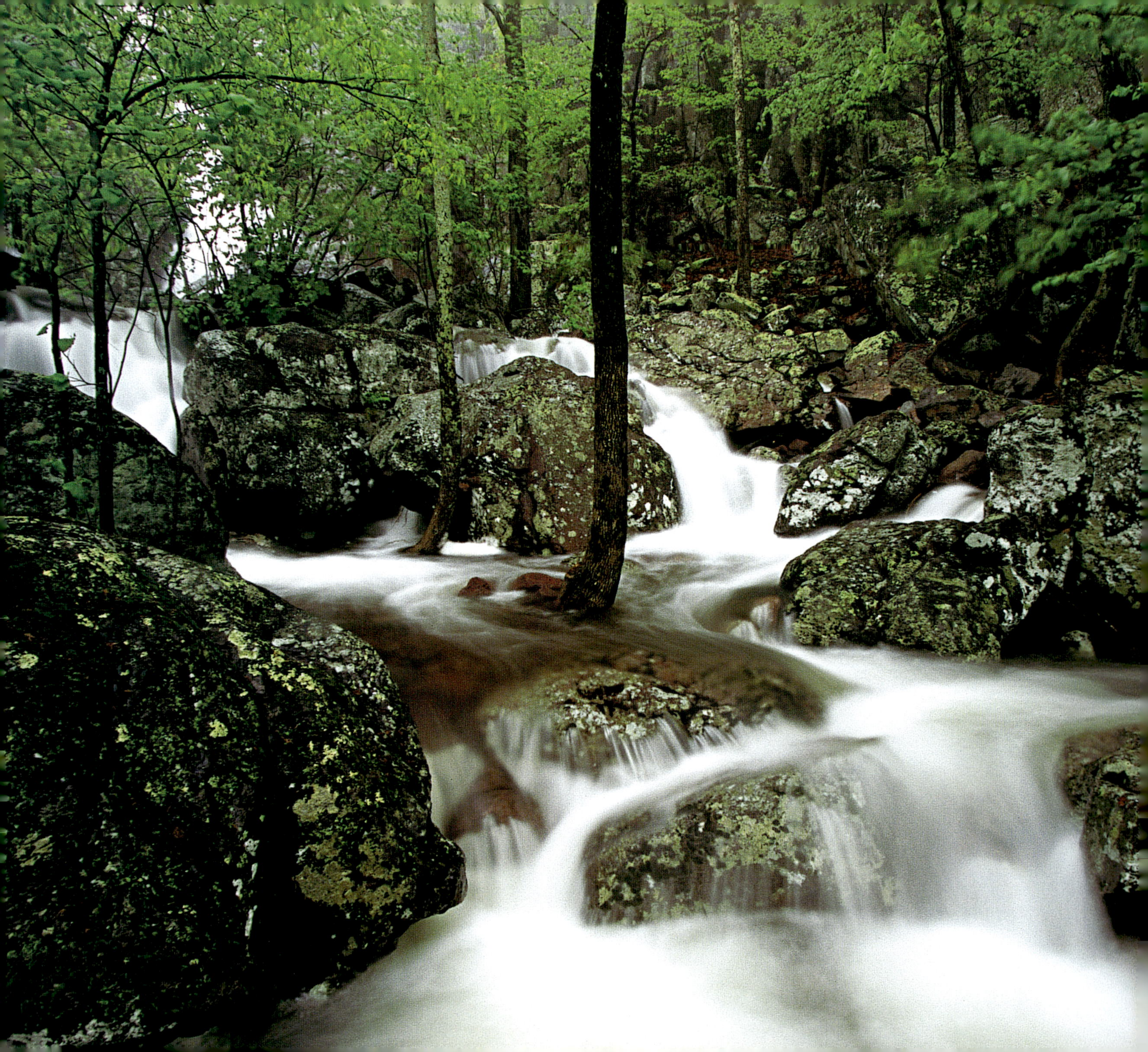

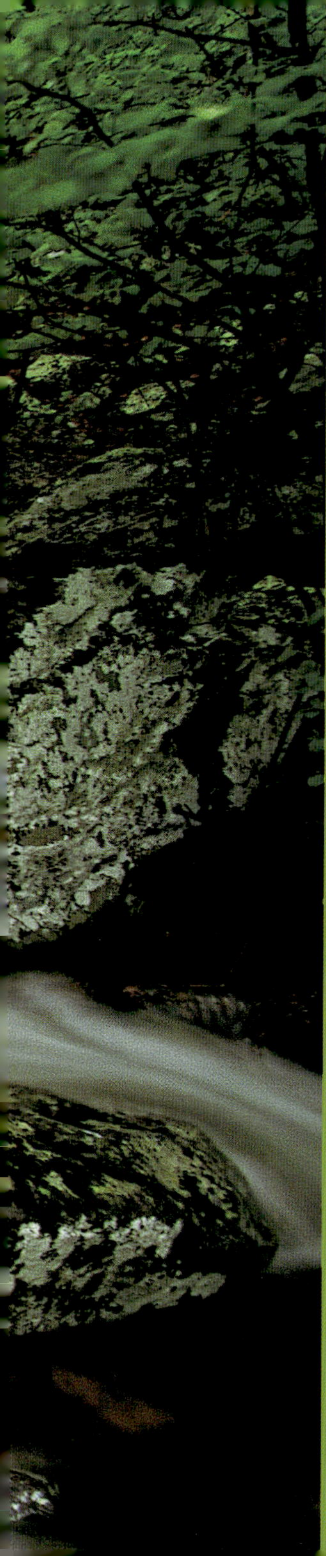

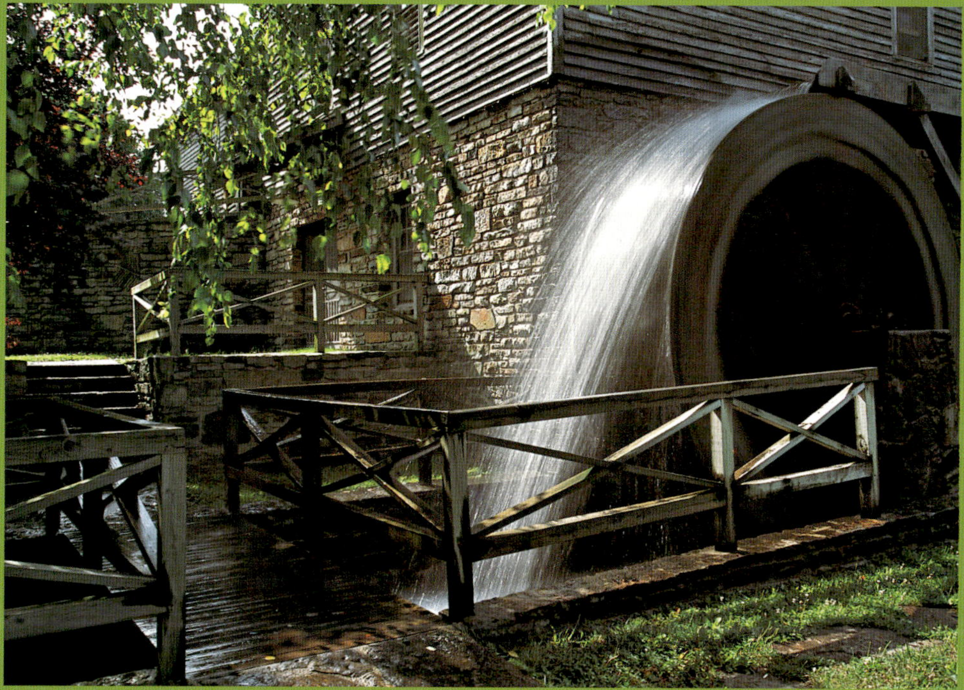

Above: In Point Lookout, the Edwards Mill uses a 12-foot water wheel to turn the grindstone to make whole-grain flours and cornmeal. College of the Ozarks students use the upstairs studio for learning to weave rugs, shawls, and other items on traditional looms.

Left: Mina Sauk Falls cascades 132 feet over rocky ledges on Taum Sauk Mountain. This large state park in the St. Francois Mountains provides access to shady, beautiful forests of oak and hickory. A footpath leads to the top of 1,772-foot-high Taum Sauk, the highest point in Missouri.

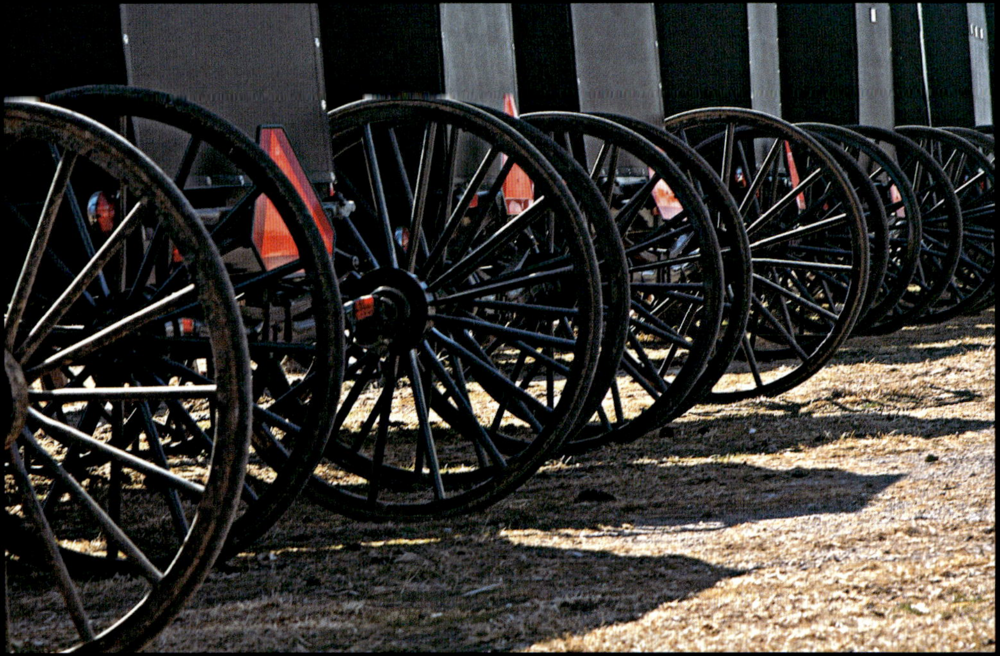

Above: Horse-drawn carriages are still in use in Morgan County. Mennonite congregations moved to this central Missouri region in the 1860s to maintain their peaceful agrarian lives.

Right: Sunrise colors the 2,200 acres of wetlands and cypress swamps protected within Otter Slough, on the St. Francis River. The area attracts thousands of migrating waterfowl; in some years, duck numbers have reached 60,000.

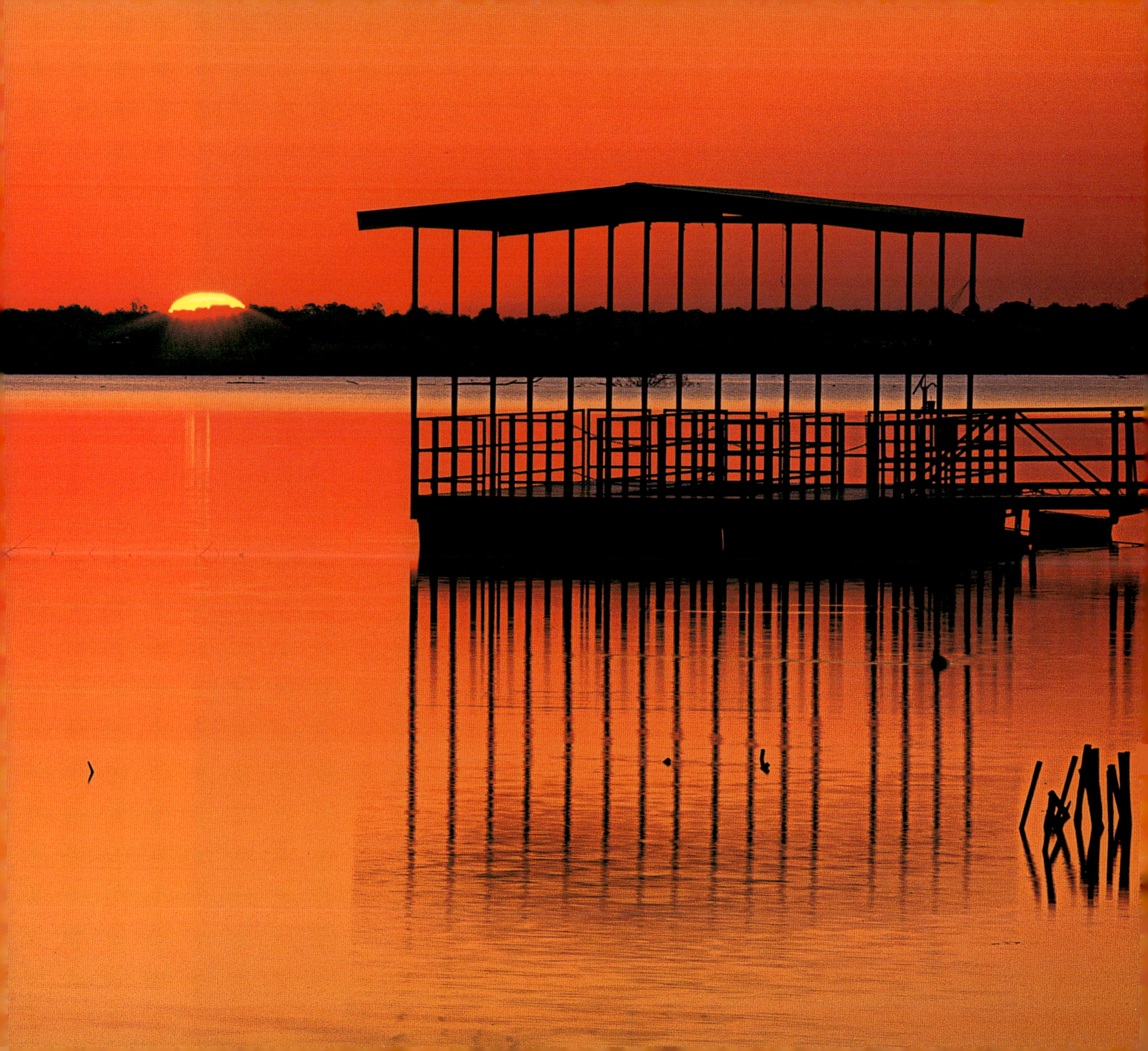

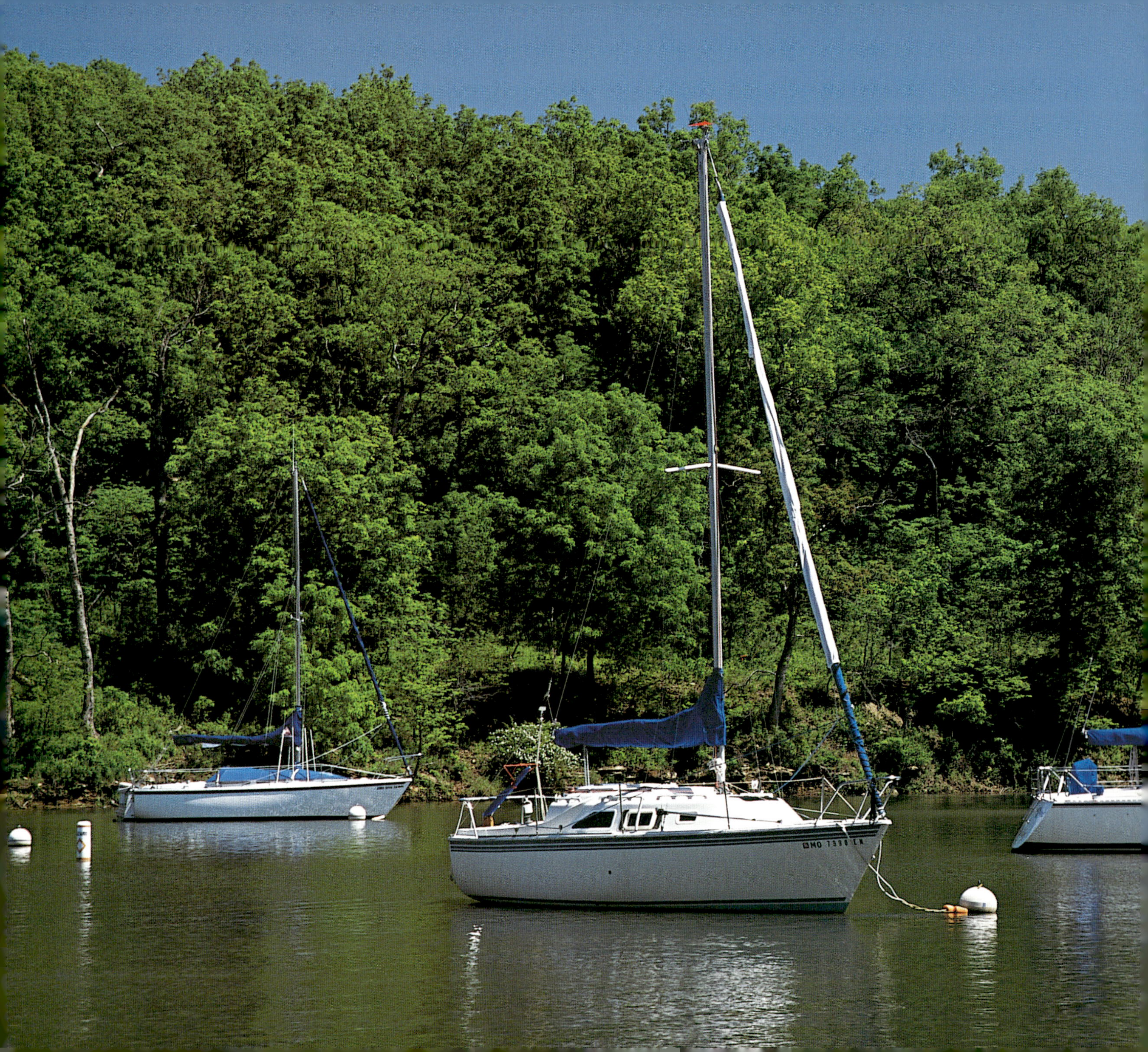

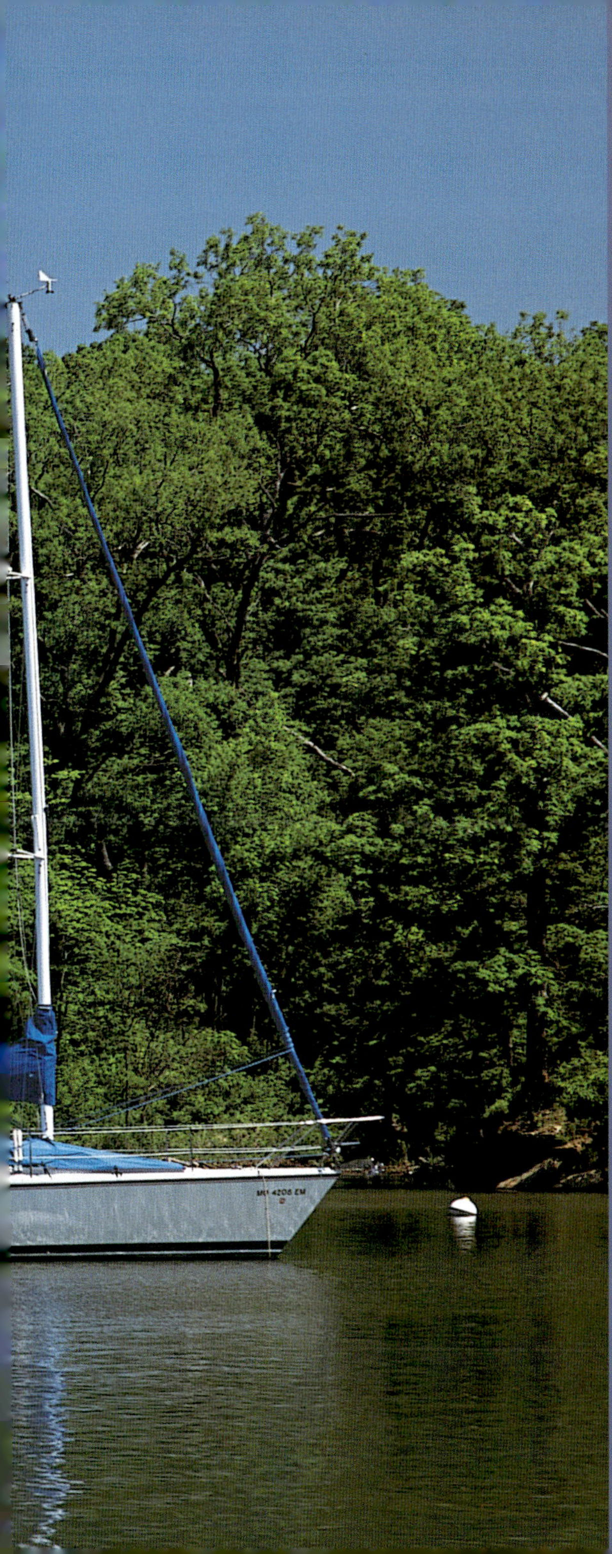

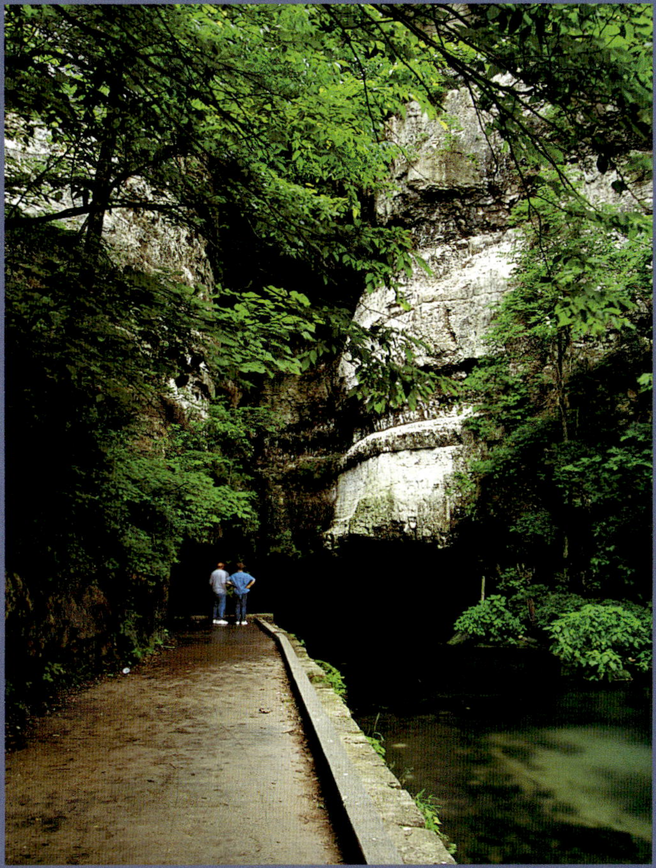

Above: Roaring River State Park encompasses nearly 4,000 acres of rocky terrain surrounding this freshwater spring. Hikers can stroll along the ten miles of trails and watch for trout in the river.

Left: Modern sailboats rest at anchor in a cove near Missouri Town 1855. Living history interpreters at Missouri Town 1855 use the original structures, furnishings, and equipment to demonstrate farm life in the mid-nineteenth century.

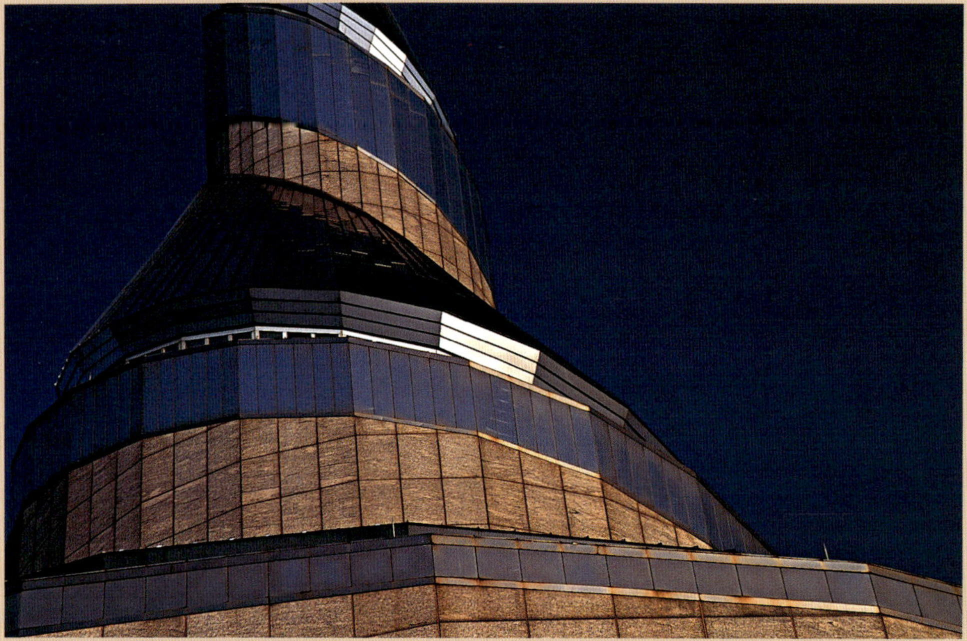

Above: The world headquarters for Community of Christ serves its members from this unique structure in Independence, built in 1993. Followers of Joseph Smith and the *Book of Mormon* split into two groups, the Church of Jesus Christ of Latter-Day Saints and the Reorganized Church of Jesus Christ of Latter-Day Saints, now called Community of Christ.

Right: Created in the early 1900s, the J. C. Nichols Memorial Fountain was moved to Kansas City in 1960 from Long Island, New York, to bring a cooling visual delight to residents entering the Plaza district. In 2006, Kansas City was named one of ten all-American cities by the National Civic League.

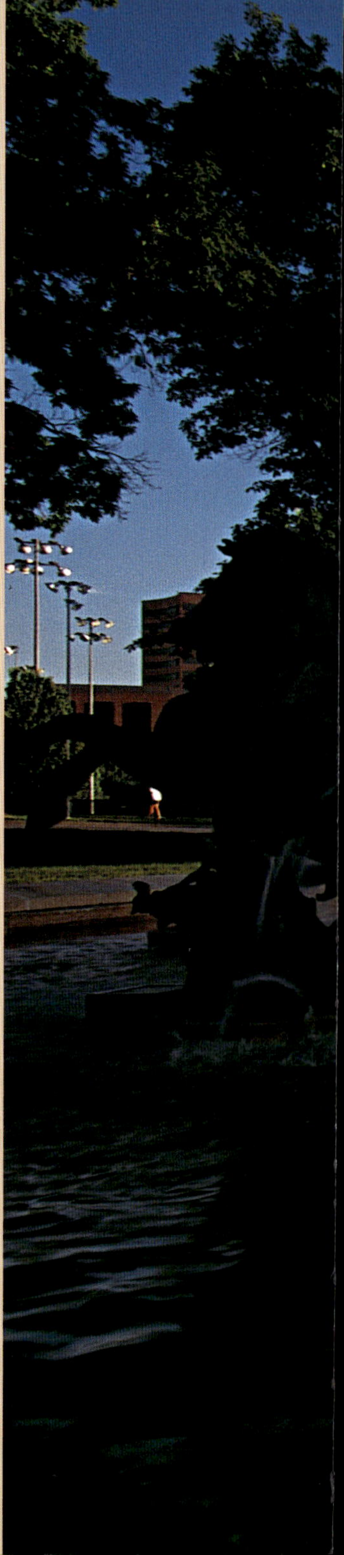

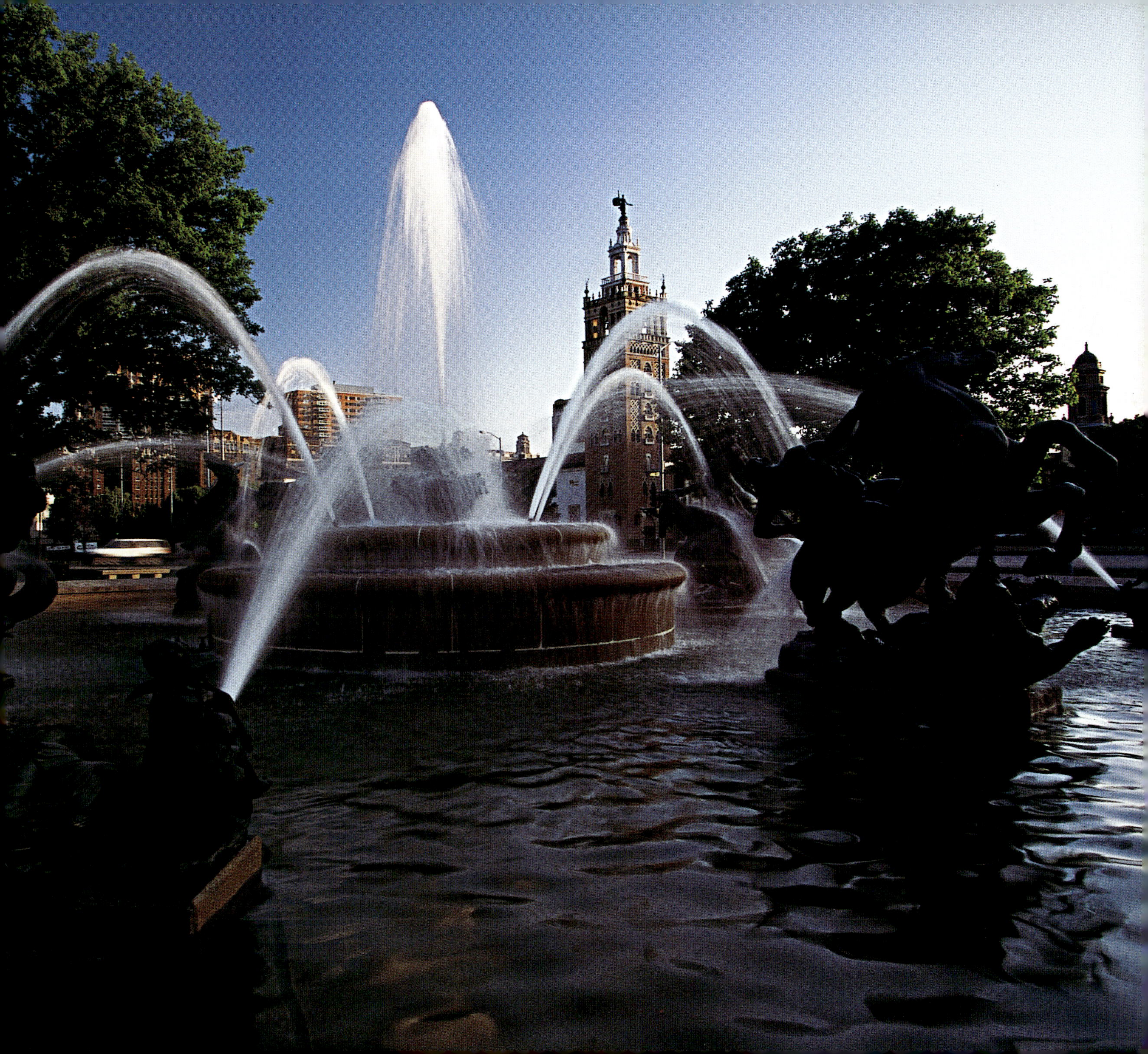

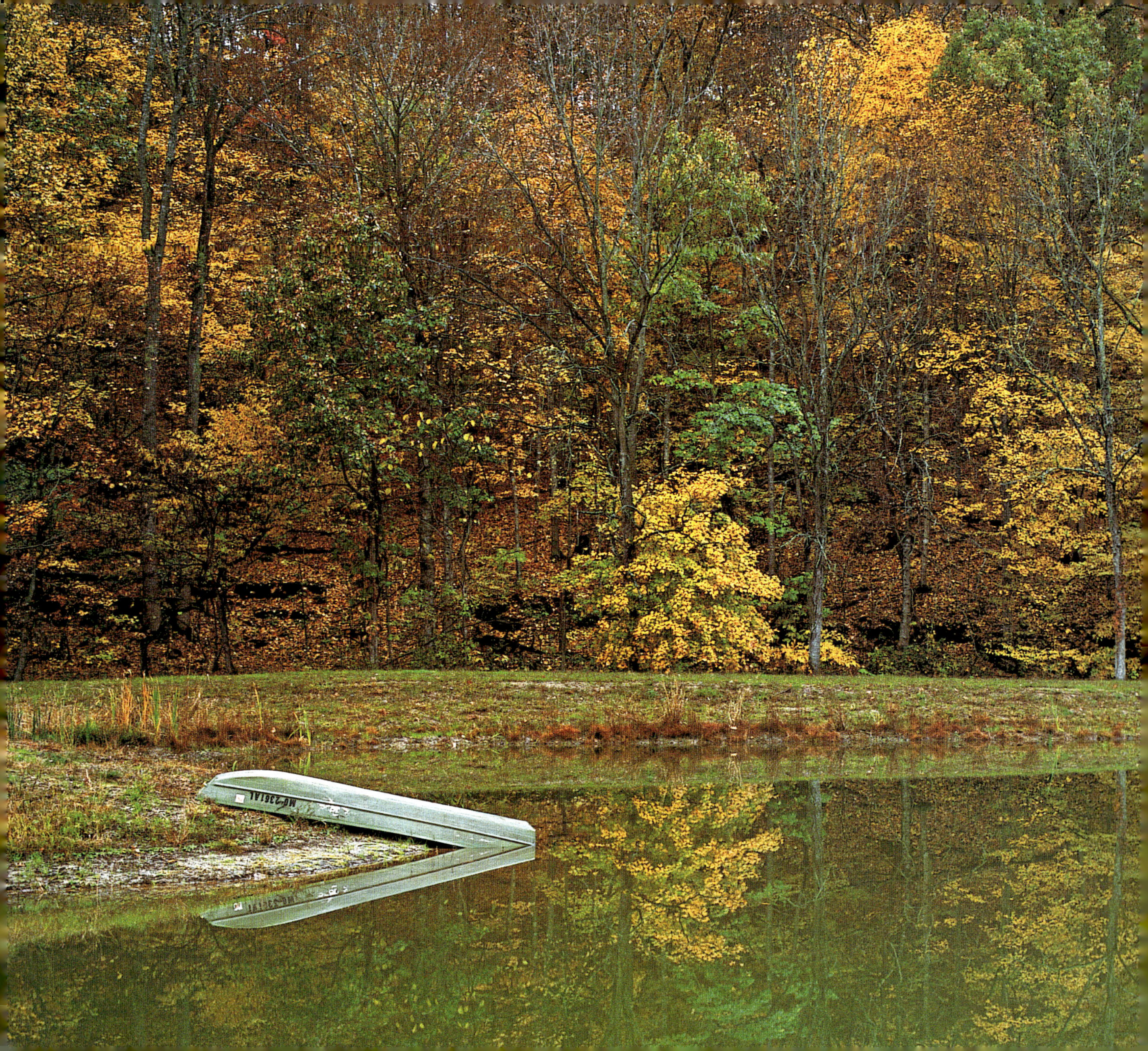
MO 2361AL

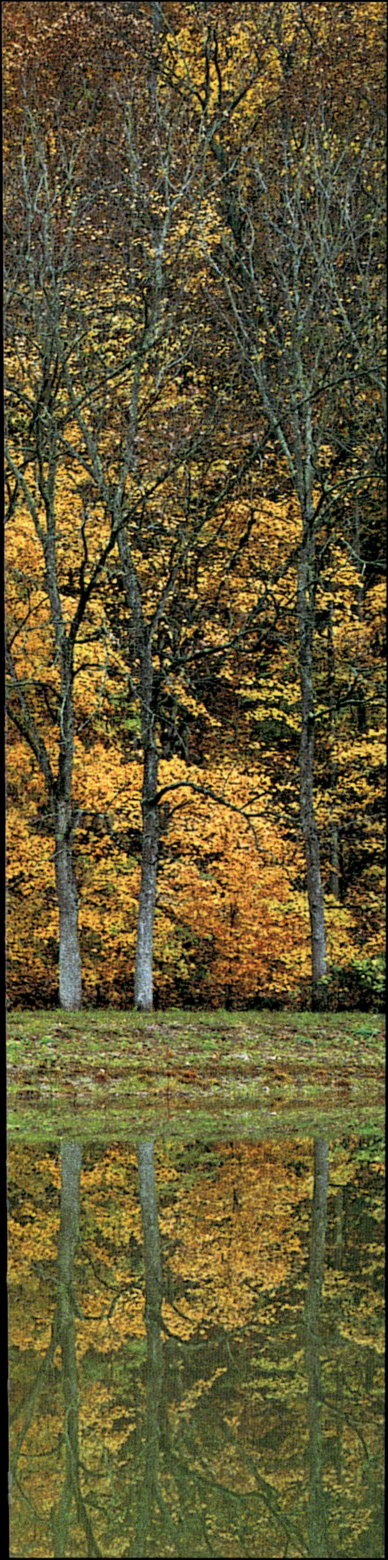

Left: A rowboat awaits another outing in a quiet pond framed by autumn hues. Missouri has 811 square miles of water in its total of 68,886 square miles.

Below: The bullfrog is Missouri's state amphibian, chosen from among 41 species of amphibians residing in the state. The largest bullfrog on record weighed several pounds and measured more than 8 inches.

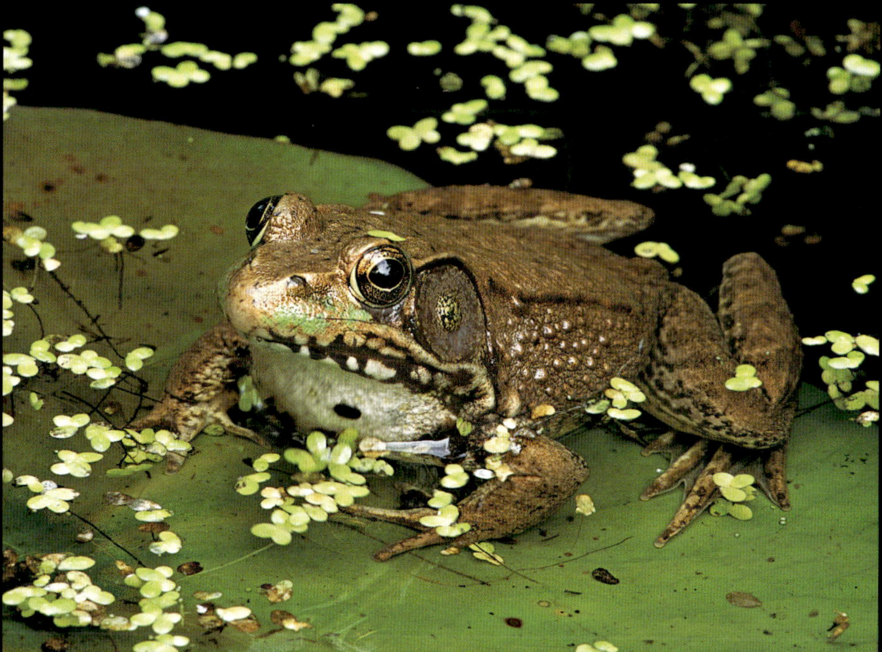

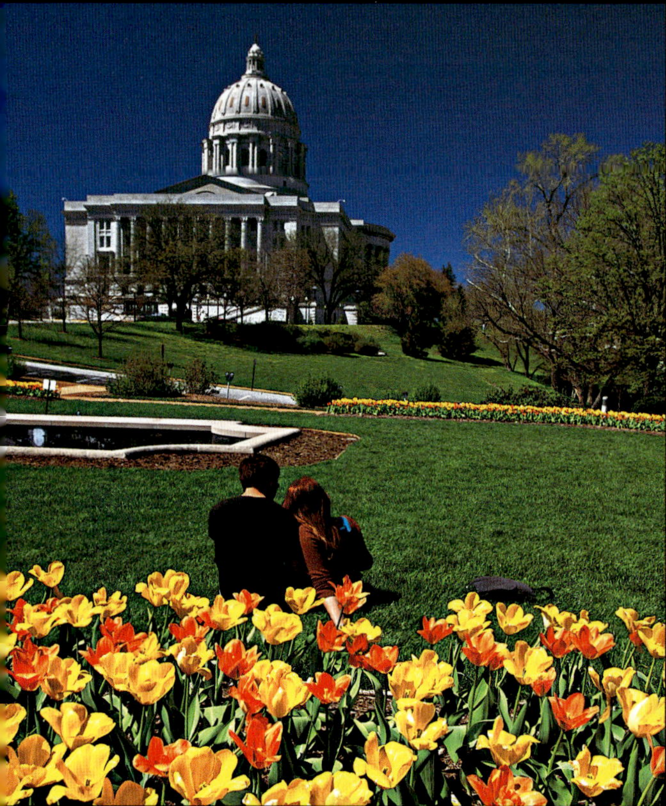

Above: Tulips adorn the foreground of Jefferson City's three-acre grounds surrounding the Missouri State Capitol, completed in 1918. Missouri was admitted to statehood on August 10, 1821. The first capitol, in Saint Charles, is now a state historic site.

Right: Dewdrops sparkle on the tips of this flower petal at Shaw Nature Reserve, part of the Missouri Botanical Garden. The reserve features native flora and fauna, as well as a replica of a traditional sod house, and the impressive Bascom House, built in 1879.

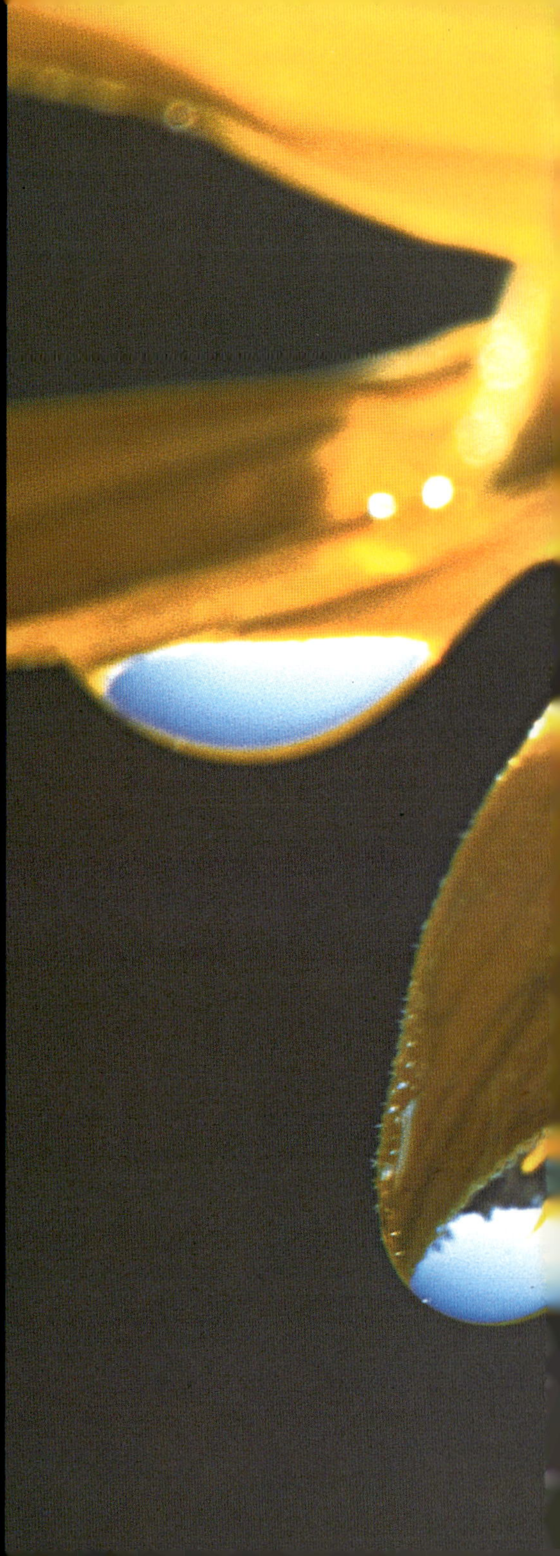

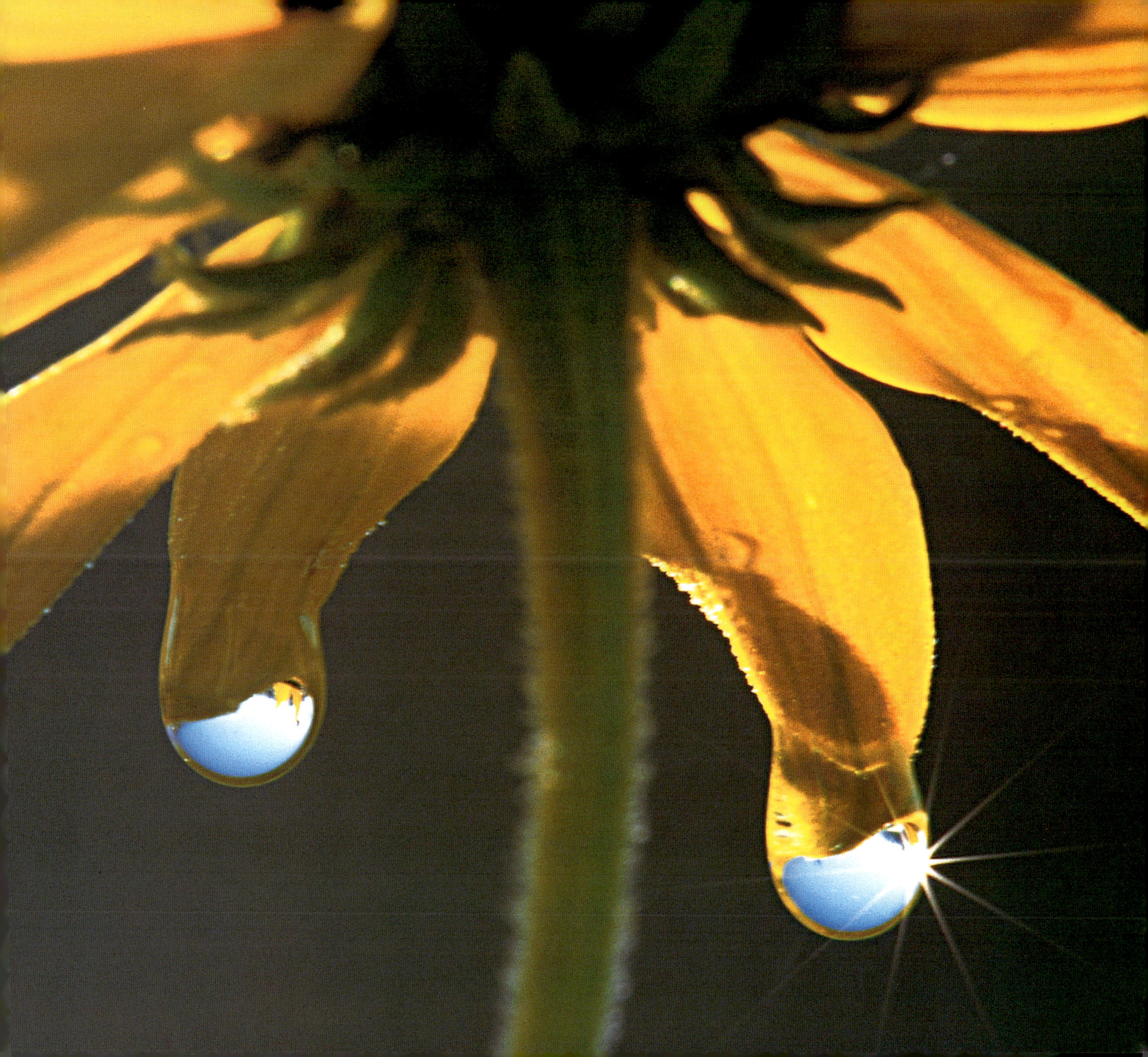

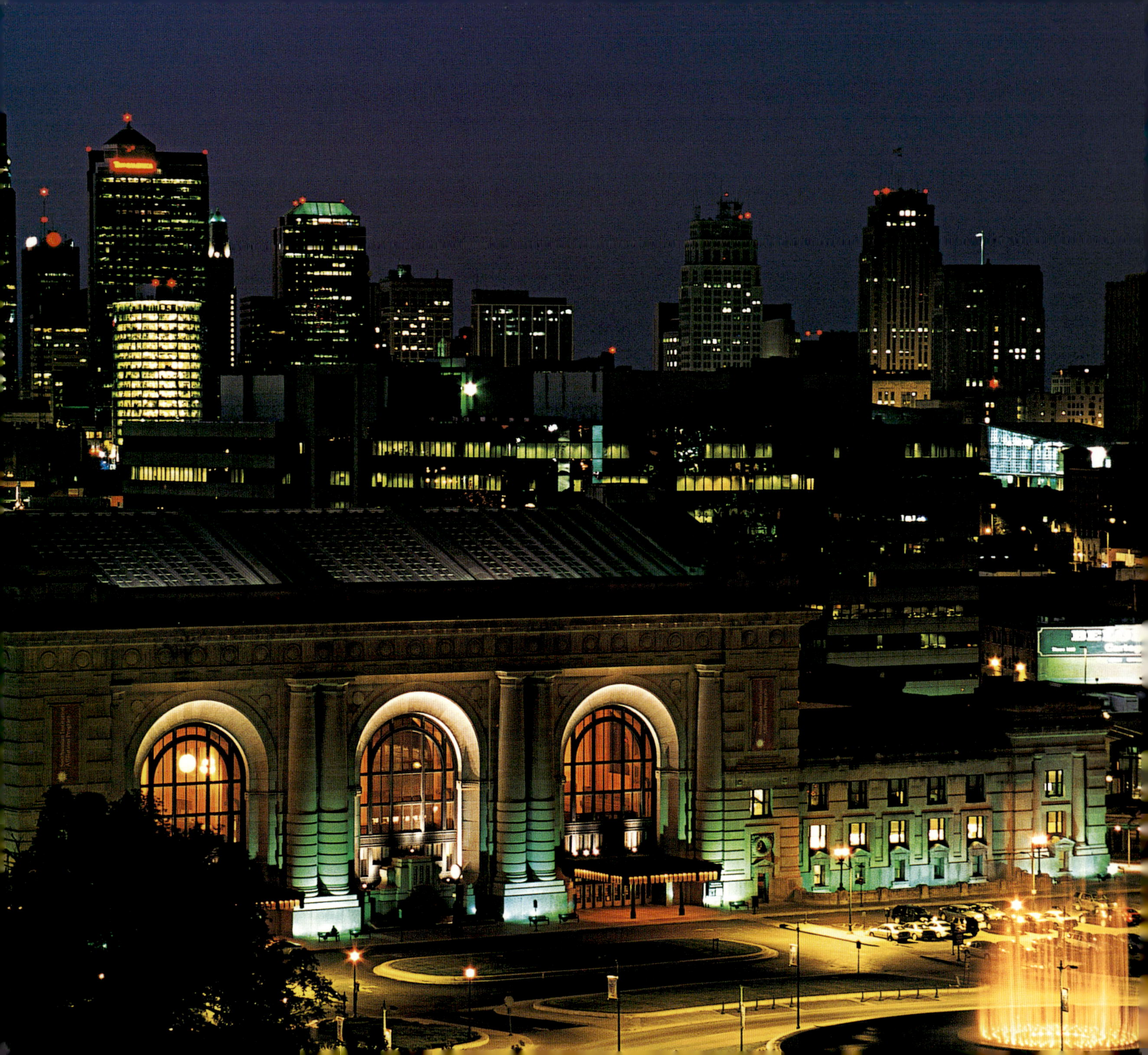

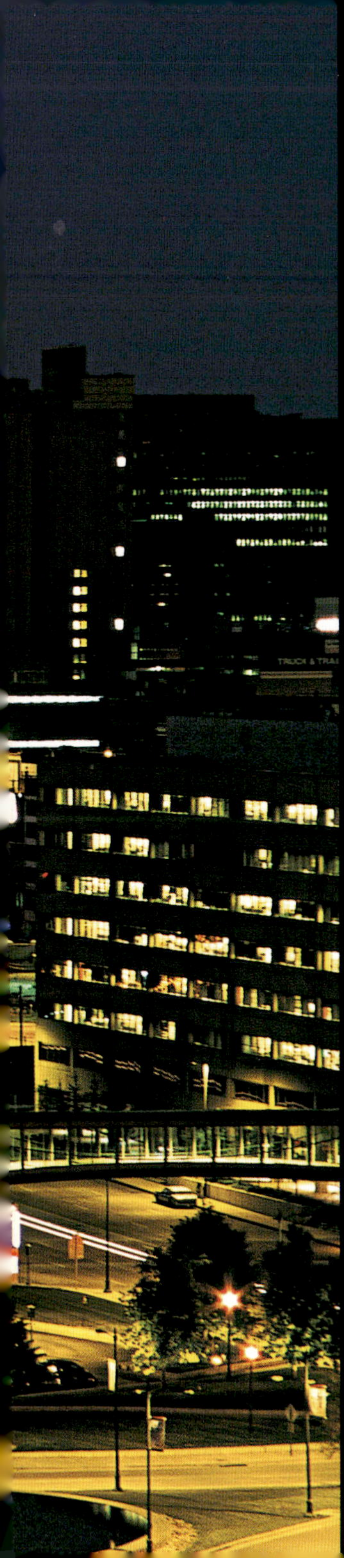

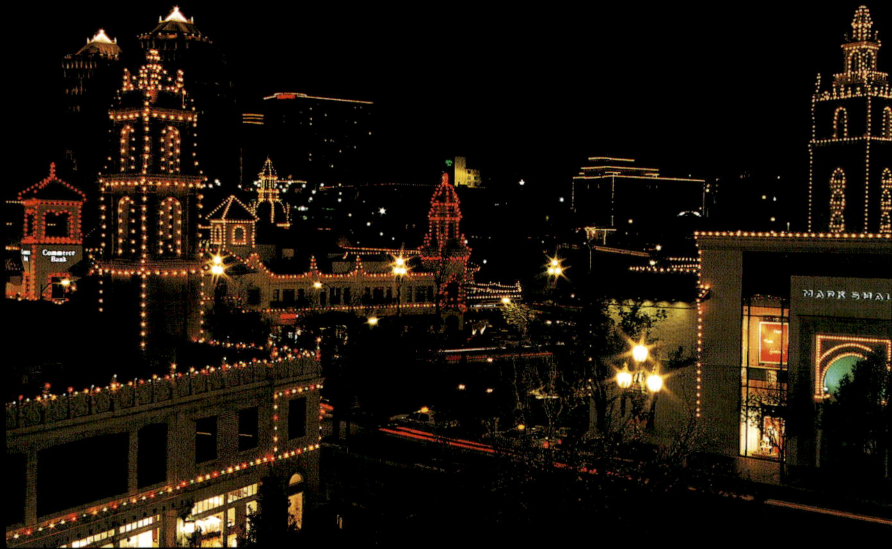

Above: Twinkling holiday light displays at Kansas City's Country Club Plaza attract people to the area's many well-known retail shops and restaurants.

Left: Restored in the 1990s, Union Station underscores the dramatic skyline of modern Kansas City. Not only can you catch the Amtrak train here, but Union Station offers more than 50 interactive activities at its Science City, as well as a planetarium, history exhibits, and live performances.

Right: Four gigantic badminton birdies landed on the lawn at Kansas City's Nelson–Atkins Museum of Art in 1994. Each shuttlecock weighs 5,500 pounds and stands nearly 18 feet tall.

Below: The six Ionic columns are the traditional symbol of the University of Missouri–Columbia. They once supported the portico of Academic Hall, the first building erected on campus, which burned in 1892.

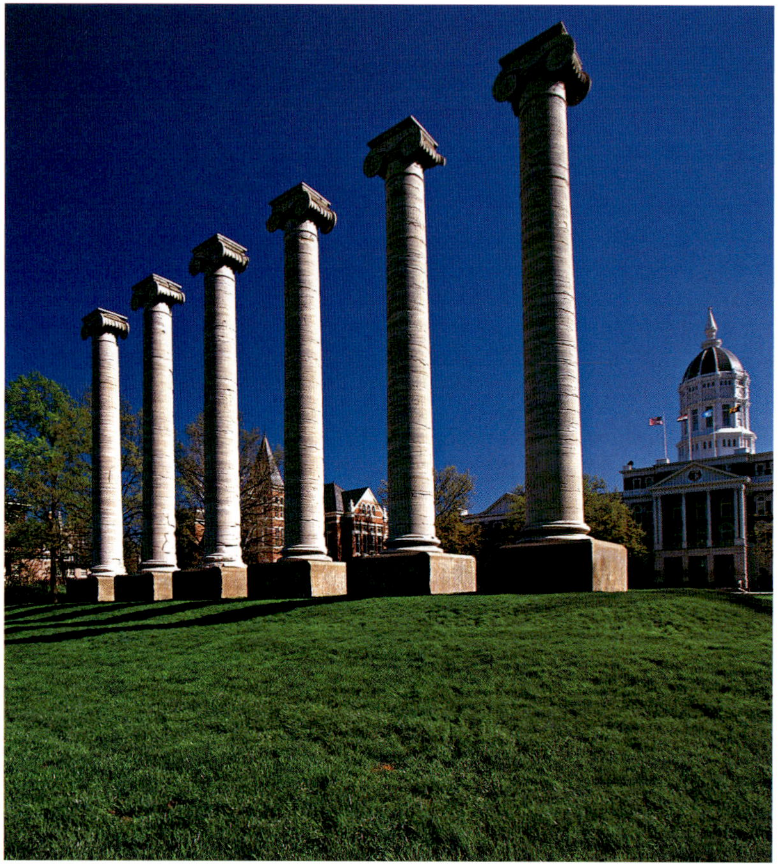

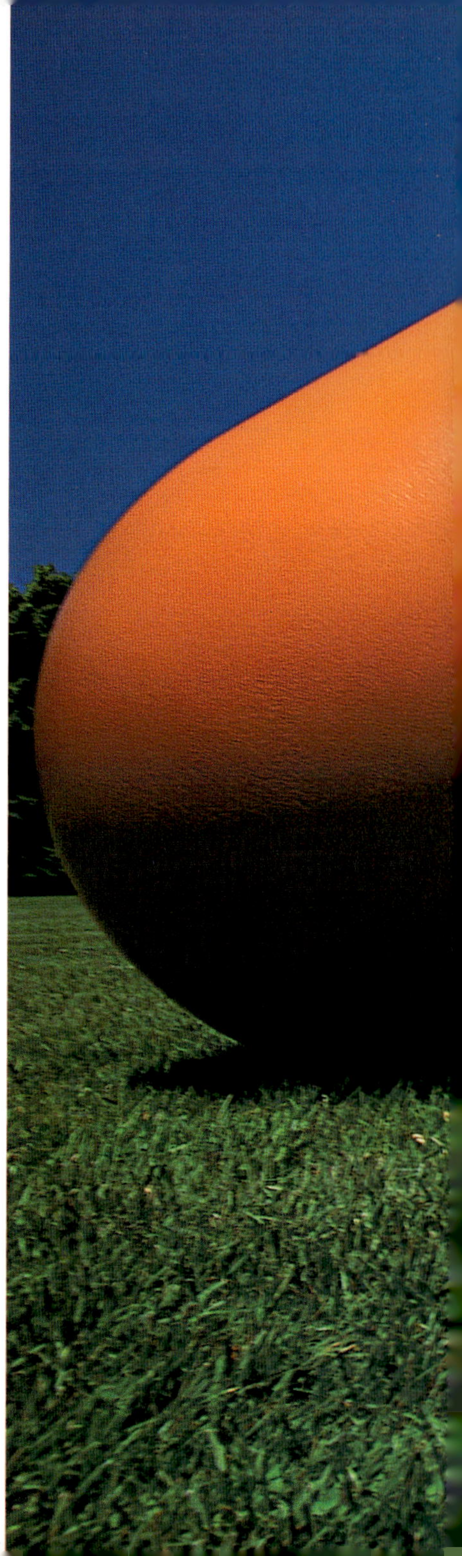

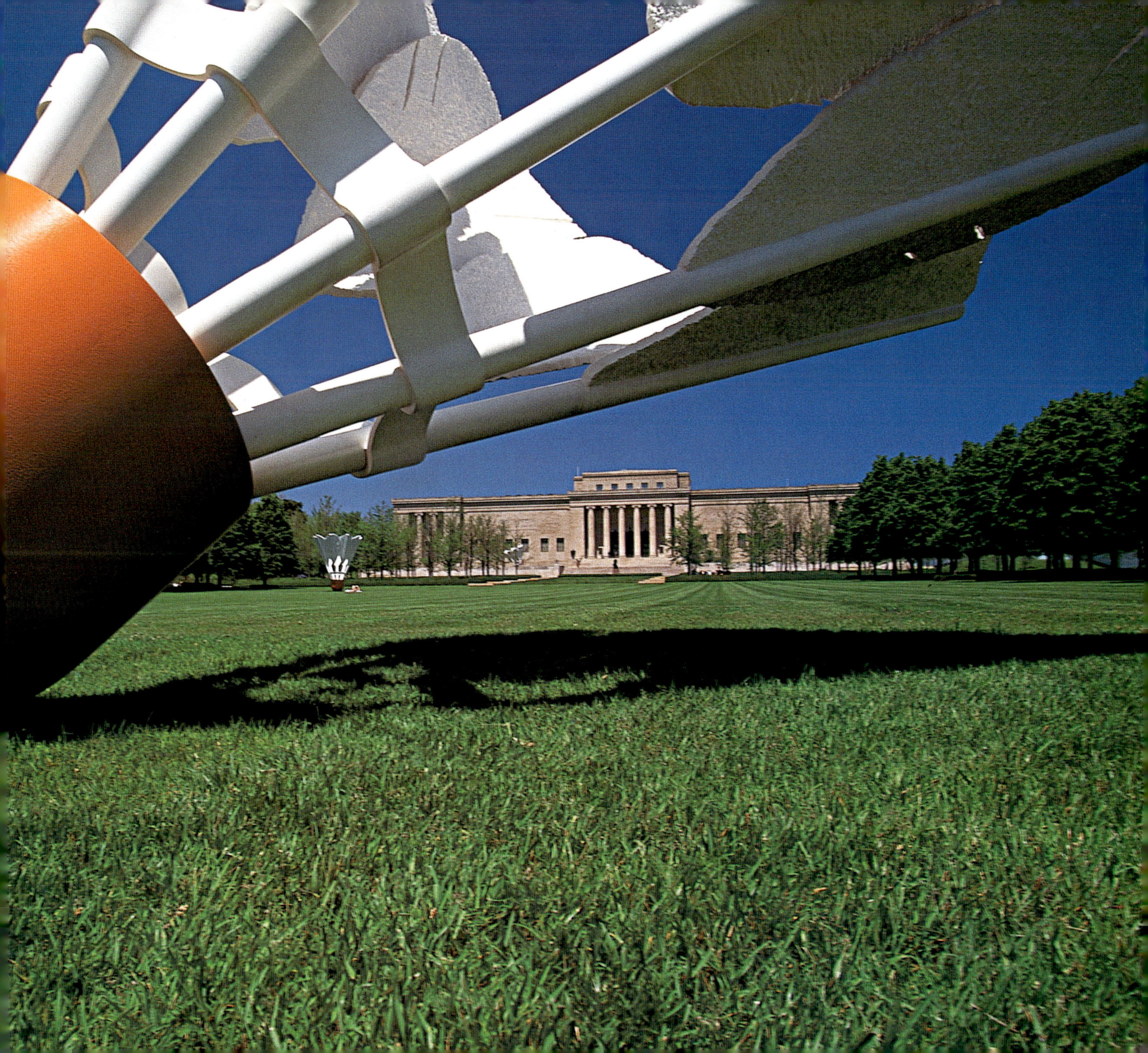

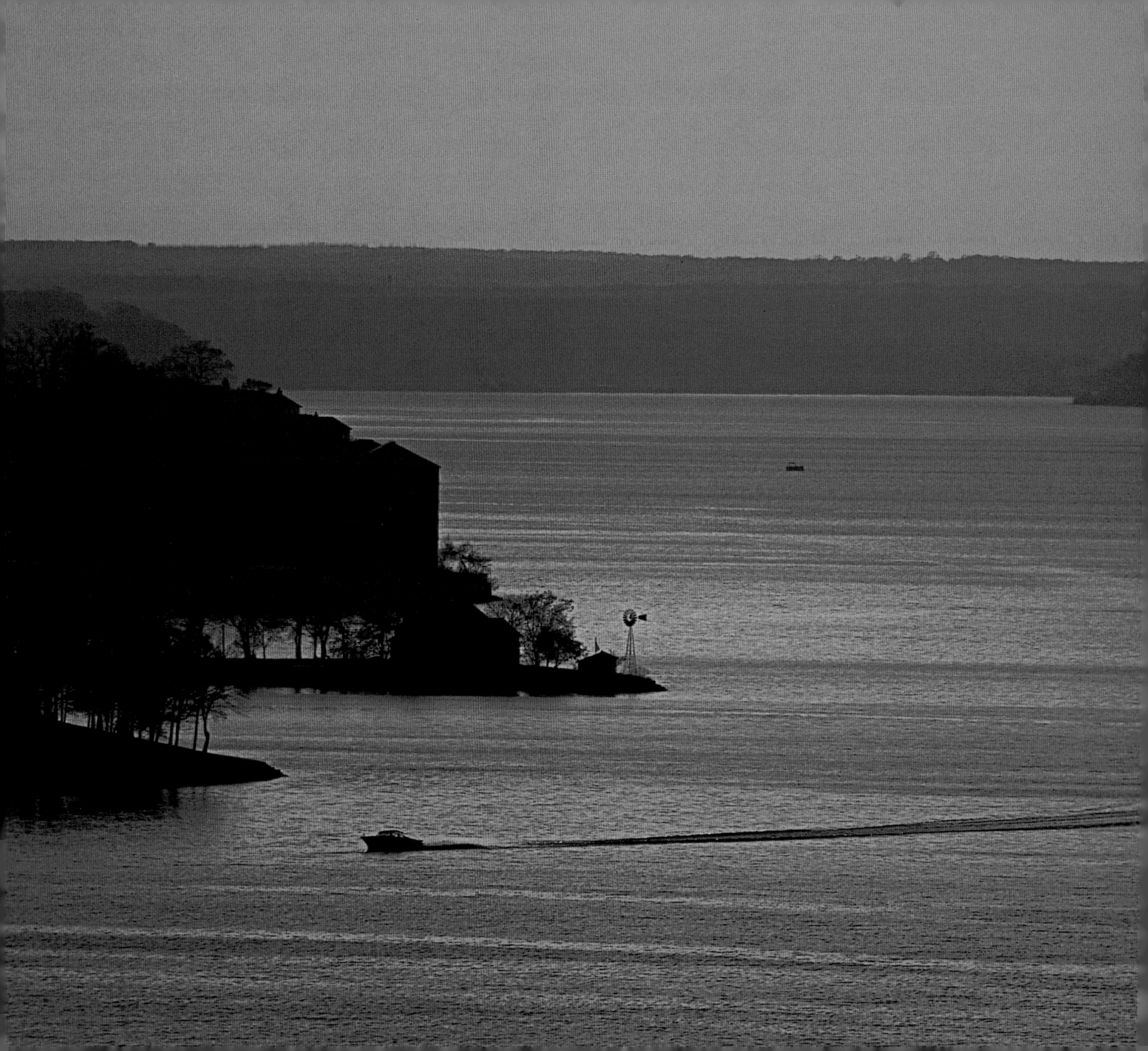

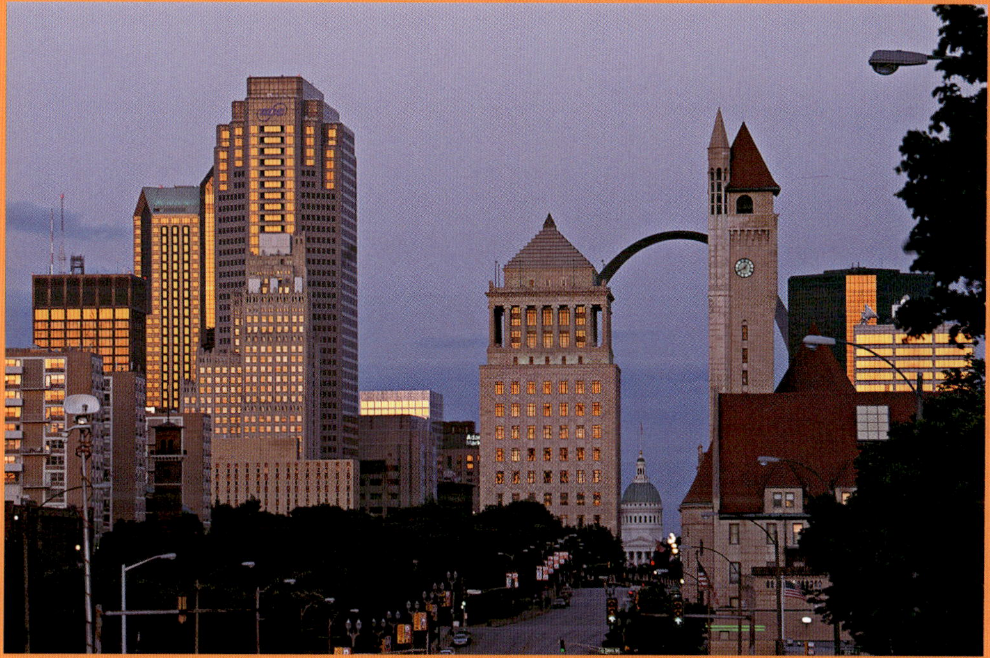

Above: This St. Louis street offers a glimpse of old and new architecture, with the Old Courthouse, built in 1828, framed under the distinctive 630-foot-tall Gateway Arch, completed in 1965.

Left: At nearly 92 miles long, Lake of the Ozarks is one of Missouri's largest reservoirs. Lake of the Ozarks State Park provides boat launches, as well as opportunities for hiking, camping, horseback riding, and other outdoor activities.

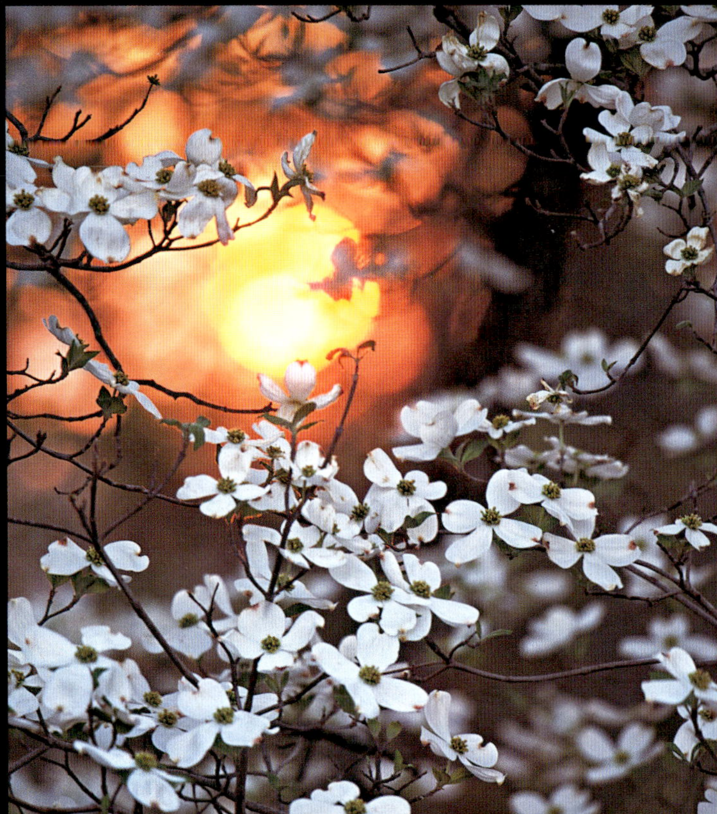

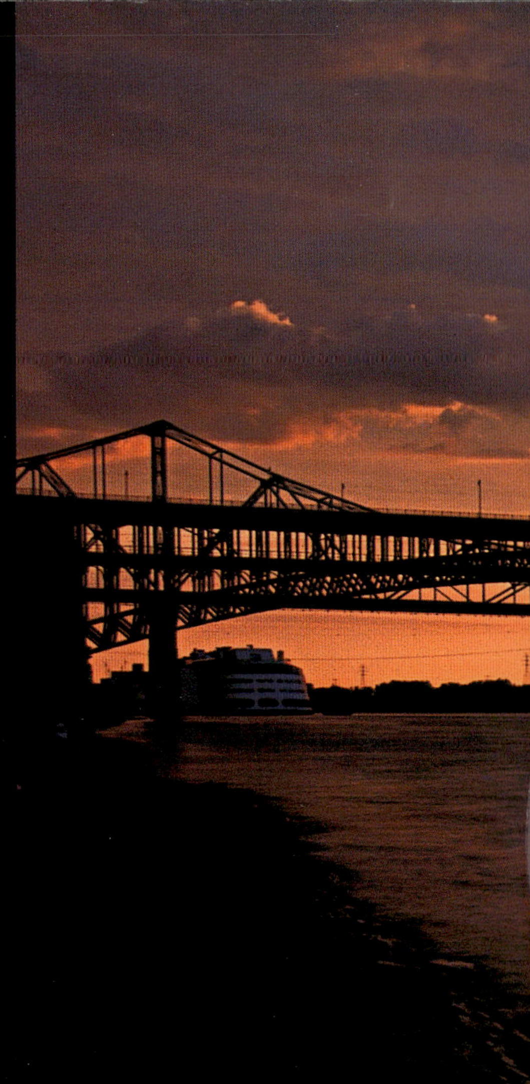

Above: Four white bracts surround each cluster of tiny, yellowish flowers on a flowering dogwood, the state tree of Missouri. In addition to the usual state emblems, such as birds and flowers, Missouri has a state grape (the Norton/Cynthiana grape) and a state musical instrument (the fiddle).

Right: Sunrise lights the Mississippi River in dramatic hues of pink, purple, and gold.